Classroom Practices in Teaching English 1978-1979

Classroom Practices
in Teaching English
1978-1979

Activating
the Passive Student

Gene Stanford, Chair,
and the Committee on Classroom Practices

National Council of Teachers of English
1111 Kenyon Road, Urbana, Illinois 61801

Grateful acknowledgment is made for permission to reprint the following material. "Daybreak" is reprinted from *The Elements of San Joaquin* by permission of the University of Pittsburgh Press, copyrighted 1977 by Gary Soto. Two untitled poems are reprinted by permission of the author, Ann Shepherd.

Book Design: Tom Kovacs

NCTE Stock Number 06889

Library of Congress Cataloging in Publication Data

Main entry under title:

Activating the passive student.

    (Classroom practices in teaching English ; 1978–1979)
    Includes bibliographies.
    1. Motivation in education.   I. Stanford, Gene.
II. National Council of Teachers of English. Committee on Classroom Practices.   III. Series.
LB106.5.A23   371.1'02   78-11561
ISBN 0-8141-0688-9

Contents

4. Getting Involved in Research

Preface

The urgency of countering the passivity that television seems to breed in today's young people became the dominant theme of the open meeting of the Committee on Classroom Practices in Teaching English held in New York City on November 24, 1977. After two hours of discussing important issues facing English teachers, the four committee members and fifteen other members of the Council agreed with Ouida Clapp that students are in danger of becoming "videots" and that the need to activate young people was at the heart of all the issues over which the discussion had ranged.

Promptly after the meeting, invitations for manuscripts on activating the passive student were issued in *Elementary English*, *English Journal*, *Council-Grams*, *College English*, and *English Education*, and in the journals of numerous NCTE-affiliated organizations. Several related journals also carried the invitation for manuscripts.

By the April 15 deadline, 164 manuscripts were submitted by educators in 45 states and Canada. This enthusiastic response, larger than that of any recent year, may be further evidence of teacher concern about and commitment to active student involvement in learning. By contrast, only half this number of contributions was generated the previous year when the committee chose to focus on "teaching the basics."

The manuscripts, with authors' names removed, were evaluated by committee members Jane Hornburger, Jeffrey N. Golub, Raymond J. Rodrigues, and the Chair—a committee representing different geographical areas and a variety of viewpoints at several educational levels.

Twenty-seven manuscripts were ultimately selected for publication and approved by the Council's Editorial Board. These approaches to activating students vary as widely as the geographical regions and educational settings in which their authors work. But they have a common purpose: to share with other teachers specific and successful classroom strategies that involve students in *doing* English, not just absorbing it.

Introduction

"He is tired; his eyes have a staring quality, not lively; he is either apathetic or hyperactive, each in the extreme," said Edward R. Stone, head of the Kimberton Farms School, in an article by Nancy Larrick that appeared in the *New York Times* recently. He was describing the child who has been watching too much television.

We have all seen them, the children of our media-centered culture, their vision extended so far by electronic means that the moon and Mars are a part of their experience, but their eyesight is so accustomed to focusing on television that the world around them has faded into a blur. We have watched them, headphones blaring a hypnotic beat and drowning out the sounds of conversation, of birds, and of crickets. These are the children that Jerzy Kosinski has dubbed "videots."

A generation ago, school was the place where children were transported to strange and far-away lands through books and stories told by their teachers. They left the school building to spend the rest of the day interacting with their peers and with their families and gaining direct experience with the real world. Today, for many, the situation is reversed. Many children spend more hours in front of the television set than they spend in school—leaving little time for contact with friends, or with the world around them.

Thus, we are faced with a generation of children whose needs and interests are quite different from those for whom our schools and traditional teaching methods were designed. As children, most of us were fascinated to read about knights and princesses, about animals and airplanes, about Eskimos and Japanese. But today, television provides information far more vividly and immediately. If we see our job as chiefly the imparting of information, we are likely to lose in the competition with television. As the old saying goes, "I hear, and I forget. I see, and I remember."

But there's yet another line to that old saying: "I *do*, and I understand." And "doing" is what television does not provide, nor even allow. The child who spends fifty hours a week watching television—seeing lions and tigers in their natural habitats, watching dolphins leap and bear cubs frolic—but who has no time to pet a dog, to feed a cat, or to cry over the death of a mouse will really understand very little of what is important. Or, as Ernest O. Boyer, United States Commissioner of Education puts it, "The child or person who is used to receiving messages but not shaping ideas will never be more than half-educated."

No one knows this more than English teachers. We learned long ago that growth in language arts comes through *doing* English, not through listening to lectures about works of literature or memorizing grammar rules. And now, faced with students whose time is increasingly given over to passive television viewing, we are attempting to develop new and better ways of actively engaging students with our subject matter. This volume presents some of the best examples of those attempts—models of how teachers have countered the passivity they observe in their students.

The approaches that the authors of these articles describe are extremely diverse. Nevertheless, it is possible to observe certain commonalities.

1. *Asking students to examine their own attitudes and feelings as well as those of others.* One author suggests having students answer questions such as, "What is something you learned about yourself as you wrote your paper?" on the day compositions are turned in.

2. *Encouraging students to produce their own work rather than merely consuming the work of others.* One author urges that students learn about poetry by writing it; another describes a procedure whereby students write their own novels.

3. *Giving students problems to solve.* Rather than telling students the facts, many teachers pose realistic problems through which students can arrive at conclusions on their own.

4. *Setting students to work in task-oriented small groups.* Many of the successful strategies reported here take advantage of the desire to interact with others by having students work cooperatively to accomplish a task.

5. *Structuring role-playing and dramatic activities.* One author put characters from a literary work on trial, with students taking appropriate roles. Other authors have also incorporated various kinds of dramatic activities into their lessons.

6. *Allowing students to make decisions about classroom organization and learning experiences.* Having decided to establish a "reading corner," one author gave students the job of planning all aspects of it, and they responded enthusiastically.

7. *Sending students into the community.* Field trips, interviews, and community-based research abound in the lessons reported here.

8. *Organizing class discussions with students taking leadership responsibility.* At least two authors report success with discussions in which all members of the class are seated in a large circle and students, rather than the teacher, have primary responsibility for leadership.

9. *Fostering student-to-student interactions to develop the communication skills needed for interpersonal relations.* One teacher suggests pairing students to interview each other. Another article reports a highly successful project in which students corresponded with one another over a period of a semester.

10. *Providing opportunities for students to help one another.* Frequently these authors capitalize on the ability of one student to help another—by critiquing papers, by preparing supporting materials for books, by sharing information.

11. *Devising educational games which combine high motivation with effective skill building.*

When one reviews the types of teaching strategies contributors most often recommended, one is struck by the extent to which they center on interaction between persons. In order to activate students, it seems that a teacher must release them from isolation in study carrels, from completing worksheets while seated at desks lined up in straight rows, from the dictum of "do your own work." Activated students are in touch with other people.

Students come alive when they are involved with other human beings, and they learn more as a result. The power of human interaction is readily seen by observing the speech patterns of children. A child from a home where a nonstandard dialect is spoken may spend six hours a day in school hearing mostly standard English, another five hours a day listening to standard English on television, and only two or three hours a day interacting with family and friends who speak the nonstandard dialect. What dialect will the child speak? Six hours of school and five hours of television cannot compete with even two hours of human contact. The child's language is that of the meaningful people in his or her life, even if the time spent with them is limited.

While the school can never compete with the home in terms of emotional attachment and significance of interaction, a classroom in which students make contact with one another gives learning more immediacy and meaning than the conventional classroom in which children are encouraged to behave like television viewers: "Listen to the program and don't talk back."

Finally, interactive lessons tend to be rich lessons in the sense that students usually learn several things at once. In a small group activity on literature, for example, students gain both knowledge of literature and improved ability to communicate with others. In a community-based research project, students acquire research and writing skills as well as a knowledge of the community.

It's not surprising, then, that English teachers responded enthusiastically when the Classroom Practices Committee announced the focus of this year's publication. They have obviously sensed that interactive approaches not only bring about improved learning but also meet the special needs of the television generation.

Gene Stanford
Director
Teacher Education Programs
Child Life Specialist Program

1 Getting Involved in Reading

Enhancing Basal Readers:
Six Creative Strategies

Nicholas P. Criscuolo
New Haven (Connecticut) Public Schools

One of the most enjoyable aspects of my position as a reading supervisor is the opportunity to visit classrooms to observe reading programs in action. By and large, the instruction is sound and carefully planned. Yet, in too many cases a dimension seems to be missing from these programs, a dimension that would help children to realize that there is more to reading than reading from a basal reader, completing an assigned number of workbook pages, and circling, underlining, and X'ing ditto sheets.

Many teachers, in their rush to complete a certain number of texts per year, overlook opportunities that would provide further reading experiences and allow children to put their newly-acquired skills to good use. If we polled elementary children on what they use in school to learn how to read, they would probably reply, "reader and workbook." And if we polled teachers on what step in the reading process they most often skip, it would probably be enrichment.

As an observer of children and their reactions to reading, I have come to believe that it's the smile, the interest on their faces, the sense of involvement that characterize a dynamic reading program. Are these types of behavior—behaviors which often cannot be measured by standardized tests—difficult for teachers to achieve with children? Hardly. Teachers need only to be aware of the many opportunities for initiating the fun-filled, creative strategies that comprise an enriched reading program.

Actions speak louder than words and the remainder of this article briefly describes six classroom-tested activities which have enhanced the reading experiences of children.

1. *Book catalogs.* Lists of trade books provide content summaries, but too often these lists are overlooked by teachers. When the class has completed a story in a basal reader, some

teachers sustain interest in that theme by using these lists to identify other books on a similar theme. After a youngster has completed one of these related books, an effective strategy is to have him or her draw a picture of a major event in the book and write a short synopsis of its contents. These are then compiled into a Book Catalog with an attractive cover and placed in the Interest Center or Reading Corner so that pupils in the class can "shop around" for a good book to read.

2. *Pupil specialists.* Many stories in basal readers can be used to encourage individual pupils to acquire more specialized information that will enhance their own knowledge and can also be shared with their classmates. Teachers simply note the subjects or themes that children will be reading about on future dates and develop a topic calendar. For example, in a few weeks the class will be reading one story about the life of Clara Barton and one story that takes place in Chile. Individual children then choose an area related to one of those topics, research it, and submit the results of their works as an oral or written presentation, or an artistic display. One child might make a mural depicting the major events in Clara Barton's life; another might construct a plaster-of-paris model of a typical Chilean village. When the stories in the basal reader are read, the "pupil specialists" share their research and broaden the class's knowledge of the topic at hand. Some teachers place the written reports in the Reading Corner for other pupils to read.

3. *Scenarios.* After children have finished a story in their basal readers, they will enjoy dramatizing it. This can be accomplished easily by asking the children to think of the major scenes in the story and the characters who were in them. The teacher can sketch out the play with the children by writing on the board: *Scene Number*, *Location* and *Action.* As a group, the children can rough out the outline of the play by filling in the needed information under each heading. Parts can then be assigned to individual children and, depending on the interests of the group, dialogue can be written for each scene or done ad lib. If the play is to be a "major production," the artistic talents of the children can be utilized in the construction of scenery and costumes.

Incidentally, the outline can be used as a seatwork activity for other stories. It is a good exercise in reading for detail, for main ideas, and for sequence as well as providing practice in summarization.

4. *Invented circumstances.* Opportunities exist within the framework of a basal reading program for children to write creatively about what they read. Teachers can ask children to think about the major characters in a story and then to write about what might have happened to those characters if the circumstances or locale had been different. Students can also write about what might have happened to a character after the story ended.

Fanciful stories are particularly appropriate for getting children to write. For example, some teachers list on the board several Story Starters related to the stories read in class and ask the children to complete them:

A. One day the two kangaroos decided to take a bus downtown.

B. On a hot afternoon the grizzly bear decided to stroll down Main Street.

C. The Martian knocked on Mrs. Greene's door.

Some teachers vary this activity by using an "add-to-the-story" technique which works best in reading groups or teams. A child adds a sentence to a given first line and then passes the paper to the next pupil who adds his or her sentence. Everyone has input, and some real "masterpieces" have been created this way!

5. *Book closings.* Teachers customarily go on to the next book in the series the day after a basal reader has been completed by the reading group. I suggest teachers spend a few days conducting a variety of enrichment activities before moving on. For example, children can be asked to rate individual stories in the book after they have established criteria for such a rating. They can prepare brief descriptions of story characters and, without divulging their identities, ask their classmates to identify the character they are describing. They can divide cumulative word lists into categories such as *Things to Eat, Feelings, Things to Wear.* Additionally, chil-

dren can sharpen oral reading skills by preparing a short selection from a favorite story to tape.

Teachers report success at a "book closing" by putting the following on the board: *Name, Type of Person, Reason.* Children are asked to name various story characters from stories read, to select a good word (i.e., "sympathetic," "affectionate," "belligerent") to describe each character, and to support that choice by citing a specific incident in the story.

So much can be done to enhance the enjoyment of a basal reader; what's done *after* reading the book can be as important as what's done *while* reading it!

6. *Armchair travelers.* Stories in basal readers are set in a variety of locales. A great deal can be done to bring these places alive for children. Travel agencies will supply posters, maps, and other materials. Children can prepare an illustrated lecture on a country where a particular story takes place using postcards, slides, and magazine pictures. A poster can be used as a dramatic backdrop to the presentation. Some teachers use a large map to chart out story locations. Pieces of yarn are extended from the country read about to a file card on which is written a synopsis of the story. Up-to-date information on a particular location can be obtained by asking pupils to clip out newspaper articles which discuss current events in that country.

So much can be done to enrich the basal reading program. The strategies outlined here not only enhance important reading skills, but involve young readers in active and creative pursuits and increase their enjoyment of reading immeasurably.

The Slide-Tape Review and the Reader Support Kit

Robert C. Small, Jr.
Virginia Polytechnic Institute and State University

Donald J. Kenney
Blacksburg Middle School

The young adult novel, once the pariah of literature classes, is being accepted by more and more language arts teachers and librarians. Such well-written and thought-provoking books as Lipsyte's *Contender* and Cormier's *Chocolate War* are not only read by students for their own pleasure but welcomed into the classroom as appropriate fare for study and discussion. Such junior novels are a useful means of involving students, especially those on the middle-school level, in their own education. Asking students to select an adult classic for study often proves frustrating for teacher and class, and both recognize that the request has the appearance rather than the reality of student participation. Allowing students to select a junior novel for their in-common reading, however, can be a meaningful experience for all involved. Students know the authors and types of books under consideration and are able to examine reviews of the books themselves and make quick but reliable judgments about which ones they wish to read together and discuss. Equally important is the fact that students bring to such novels as *Are You in the House Alone?* (Peck) and *One Fat Summer* (Lipsyte) a background of experiences which enables them to understand and discuss the works without the excessive help from the teacher that the classics require. (See Robert Small, "The Junior Novel and the Art of Literature," *English Journal* [October 1977] : 56-59.)

To a considerable extent, despite recent acceptance into the language arts classroom, young adult novels continue to be individually selected and read by the teenagers for whom they are written. While this state of affairs obviously reflects student involvement of a high order, the special characteristics of these novels also make it possible for students to become experts in relation to them and, therefore, to assist other students in selecting and reading books in this genre.

Selection: The Slide-Tape Review

When middle-school students consult someone about a novel to read, they often turn to their friends: "What are you reading? Is it any good?" The replies, carrying as they do the authentic teen-age voice, are more persuasive than adult suggestions. A circle of friends, however, has a limited familiarity with the many books that are available. Of course, English teachers and librarians can also make recommendations, but students often find these suggestions less than satisfactory. What is needed, therefore, is an organized collection of book reviews *by* students *for* students. Teachers have, of course, traditionally required oral and written book reports, but for many reasons such exercises have probably been more harmful than helpful. Instead, English teachers and librarians can compile a central collection of reviews of currently popular and older but worthy young adult novels without the negative characteristics of the assigned book report and make such a collection available to all students.

While such reviews might be written by students and kept on file in the library, a more stimulating and effective approach is to put such reviews into slide-tape presentations. Offered in the voice of one teenager talking to another, such reviews are immediate, personal, and convincing. Several steps are involved in the process:

1. As a part of their work in selected English classes, students choose and read or reread young adult novels which they feel will be enjoyed by other students. The teacher and librarian may, of course, suggest books, especially new ones, that they feel should be reviewed. The final choices, however, are left to the students.

2. Each student then writes a review, addressed to other students, designed to last several minutes when delivered orally. After revision, the student tapes an informal version of that review. The reviewer also determines the content for 6-12 slides to accompany the review. These slides may show the student-reviewer reading the book, the book itself, or people and places similar to those in the book.

3. The slide-tape package is filed in the school library. The cards in the card catalog and the books themselves are marked with a symbol to show that a slide-tape review is available.

4. When a student wishes to make use of a review, he or she checks it out from the library circulation desk and goes to a carrel equipped with a tape player and slide viewer.

This collection of reviews grows rapidly as students and teachers come to see its worth, but the expense can be shared by the school, the English department, and the library; indeed, students are often willing to supply the tapes and slides themselves when they realize that their reviews are part of the school library and will be used by other students for years to come.

While the primary users of such reviews are students, language arts teachers will also use them in several ways:

1. To help a class select a book from several under consideration for in-common reading

2. To introduce a specific book selected for in-common reading

3. To preview several novels on the same theme or of the same type (such as science fiction), particularly when a unit on that theme or type is to be introduced

4. To prepare students for a class visit to the library

The school librarian will also use these reviews as a part of various library lessons and in the presentation of new books. A particularly effective strategy is to establish a "new books" station in the library where slide-tape reviews are set up for immediate use. Such a station, with titles changing regularly, can become a popular feature to which students go directly when they visit the library.

Reading: The Reader Support Kit

When a student has selected a young adult novel to read, the helping involvement of peers does not have to cease. While teenagers bring to the junior novel much of what is needed for enjoyment and understanding, there are activities that they can carry out before they begin to read, during their reading, and after they have finished that will enhance the impact of the book. Students who have read and enjoyed a particular junior novel, working alone or in small groups, can ask themselves what a reader might do before reading the book that would help in understanding the book. They can look for ways to help a prospective reader think about the problem the novel presents and to encourage a receptive frame of mind. In addition, student experts on the work can reflect on what subsequent readers might do that would strengthen and deepen their response to the book. After preliminary help from their teacher on how to analyze a book in order to develop such activities (see Robert Small, "Preparing To Teach a Novel," *High School Journal* 57 [1974]: 190-203), students can go to work preparing Reader Support Kits to accompany popular young adult novels.

While some packages may consist of written materials such as assignments or copies of newspaper and magazine articles, the more effective Reader Support Kits contain a wealth of materials designed to move new readers into the proper context for the novel they are about to begin—pictures, puzzles, questionnaires, appropriate objects. Prospective readers may, for instance, be encouraged to examine pictures of themselves as young children; to interview very old people in their neighborhoods; to visit specific places; to hold, feel, and examine an object like a shotgun shell; to ask themselves certain questions (see Robert Small and Donald J. Kenney, "The Adolescent Novel as Working Model," *ALAN Newsletter* [Winter 1977]: 4-6).

Invented, collected, written, and refined by students with the help of the English teacher and the librarian, such a Reader Support Kit can be checked out from the library along with the novel. While the activities in such packages are, of course, merely suggestions and a particular reader may not feel the need to carry out any of them, the activities have come from other students who have read the novel and are more likely to be carried out than teacher-assigned activities.

Reader Support Kits and Slide-Tape Reviews are ways one student can say to another, "I've read this book, and I'd like to share my experience with you. If you do some of these things, you'll like the book a lot more and get a lot more out of it." Students can guide their peers towards a successful encounter with literature and, at the same time, deepen their own experience with books. And they can also further teachers' and librarians' understanding of the relationship between teenager and novel.

The Reading Corner
That the Class Built

E. Kathleen Booher
Livingston College of Rutgers University

Before my second year of teaching began, I decided that a paperback reading corner was to be one of my classroom's "bare essentials." Knowing that funds could be slow in coming, I decided to forego a formal request to my principal and finance it myself, that is, with the help of my seventh graders.

A week before school began I went in to open windows and freshen my classroom. I fully intended to set up the reading corner so it could serve as an inviting greeting for my new students. But as I sat in that quiet classroom that would soon be buzzing with activity, I realized that part of the fun in having this corner had been the *planning* for it. Why shouldn't my students share that pleasure?

That insight turned out to be no small one. I had two seventh-grade "blocks" of thirty students—each meeting in my room for two hours a day to study English and social studies. Both groups greeted my idea with great enthusiasm, and their imaginative suggestions were endless. My own ideas now seemed restricted. I knew I could get the books inexpensively at a nearby used book store, but beyond that, my imagination had been limited.

Through much excited class discussion we decided that we must work on three issues:

1. We needed funds and a policy for acquiring paperback books.

2. We needed to agree on a decorative theme for the corner and acquire the materials to embody it. (I'd never even considered that one!)

3. We needed to establish policies for the operation and maintenance of the corner.

Like experienced financiers, my sixty students agreed that they would like to contribute books they had already read from their

11

own shelves and establish a "kitty" to which they could contribute small change. To my surprise (and happily so), no one even mentioned any "requirements." The system was to be entirely voluntary and would continue throughout the year so new books could broaden the selection. I was chosen to collect the funds and keep track of individual contributions. I would also do the book shopping on Saturday mornings, sometimes taking along a willing helper.

With that settled we discussed how much we wanted to pay for books. The used book store stocked paperbacks galore and sold them for fifty, twenty-five, or fifteen cents, depending upon their condition. The fifteen cent bargains lacked front covers. Again, to my surprise (since I had suspected that students often chose books "by their covers"), the overwhelming answer was, "Buy the fifteen cent ones so we can get more. After all, we can *make* new covers!" Which they did, faithfully, the entire year, whenever another grocery bag full of coverless paperbacks awaited them on Monday morning.

Designing the corner and then getting the materials provided students with a great sense of accomplishment. The corner became a concrete recognition of a "dream come true." They were prolific in their suggestions for a decor, and when Bryan said he could bring an aquarium, eyes lit up all across the room. Both classes approved the "marine" theme, and we soon had fishnets decorated with shells and fishing paraphernalia draped along the wall. A gurgling aquarium in the corner held an assortment of fish. The shop teacher (always a helpful friend with my students' many projects) gave us several unused boards for shelves. David's father worked in construction and brought us an ample supply of cement blocks to support the shelves. Our reading corner neared completion.

The vote for carpeting was unanimous and I shuddered, wondering from where we could expect our next "blessing." Tammy's uncle ran a carpet store. She'd see if she could get some old samples. Diane and Nick both remembered carpet scraps stored in the garage after home redecorating projects. We soon had stacks of carpet pieces in every color and texture. Laid out on the floor, they formed a beautiful patchwork pattern. But how were we to anchor them? After an unsuccessful experiment with carpet tape, Kenny suggested we nail them to a big piece of plywood. That would also make the corner "portable." Kenny's father obliged with scrap pieces of plywood cut to fit our 12′ × 12′ corner. With nails and the loan of a hammer from (you guessed it) the shop teacher, our new floor was completed. It has since endured several years of junior-high feet.

"It needs a name," Michelle suggested, and almost without discussion, a favorite emerged. Within a week a cleverly "weathered" wooden sign hung over our reading corner christening it, "The Crew's Cabin."

My seventh graders proved their ultimate responsibility in their maintenance of the "Cabin." They liked the idea of checking out books, so they set up their own system. The school librarian gave us a supply of book cards and pockets which they filled out and pasted in. The school secretary loaned us a date stamp, and students stamped their own books and filed the cards. Though we agreed on a two-week loan period, we established no penalties for overdue books. The problem seldom came up. We posted a "Schedule of Librarians," so the responsibility for reordering shelves and cleaning the corner rotated weekly and eventually included every student.

Of course, we had to decide when and how the reading corner could be used. We agreed that it should be open before and after class and during our ten-minute break. I suggested that students might use it quietly if they completed assignments while others were still working. I expected more difficulty and confusion than ever arose. Students generally read quietly on the carpeted floor or scanned new books to check out. Our only crisis, when a student's sugar cube model of an Egyptian pyramid somehow "slipped" into the aquarium, was handled without casualties. Though I'm sure our fish aged considerably in the incident, within minutes calm was restored, and an only slightly dissolved pyramid was back on display.

My students read avidly all year, and I don't recall any tendency on my part to "push them." More often, a student would come to me, book in hand, and ask what it was about. Other times, students would ask me to suggest titles I thought they might like. Sometimes I'd notice a book "making the rounds," obviously upon the recommendations of fellow students. Most of my students had grown up in our middle- to upper-middle-class, midwestern suburb and, for this reason, I had been careful to include books that would explore cultural and ethnic diversity. I was pleased when I saw even some of my less-enthusiastic readers circulating titles like *Durango Street* and *Black Like Me.*

To say the independent reading experiences of my students were positive that year is surely an understatement. But equally important was their participation in the process of realizing the corner in the first place. They shared and debated ideas, made decisions and worked to implement them. Once "The Crew's Cabin" existed, they maintained it, even after the novelty had worn off. I often thought of how much *they* would have missed and how little *I* would have learned had I set up the corner myself that previous August. What had seemed at the time only a minor change of plans allowed my students to create something they would use and respect.

As the end of the school year approached, we decided to deal with the question of what to do about the reading corner. The classes were willing to "bequeath" their collection to my future classes. But generous as they were, I wanted to remember the lesson these young people had taught me. They had worked diligently on their corner and valued it accordingly. Next year's students would have to create their own corner, suiting their own tastes and reading needs—or they couldn't appreciate the process as these students had.

I suggested we dissolve the collection and let everyone stock up for summer reading. Students could take as many books as they had contributed, either through donation or money. As fair as I thought my suggestion was, my students had one final surprise for me. Though they knew not everyone had contributed to the kitty, they wanted to divide up the collection evenly, without regard to contributor status.

With the aquarium emptied and cleaned, fishnets and shells removed from the walls, it wasn't without sentiment that I watched Michelle remove the wooden sign hanging over "The Crew's Cabin." As my seventh graders left for the summer, I thanked them for all they had taught me that year. Coming from a teacher, they thought that was rather funny. But they said goodbye with their five paperback books tucked under their arms. My room seemed barren, except for a 12′ × 12′ carpeted patch and several empty shelves waiting to begin the process again—in a new way—next year.

Literature on Trial

Karen Shawn
Lawrence Junior High School, Lawrence, New York
and Long Island University, Brooklyn, New York

"Hey, how ya doin'?"

"Hi, how are you?"

"Hi, Ms. Shawn, we missed you!"

"I missed you, too!"

We greeted each other warmly. As they took their seats, the kids began asking about my experience.

"Was it fun?"

"Did you get picked for a jury?"

"Was he guilty?"

I'd thought about telling them everything that had happened during my two weeks on jury duty, maybe adding a few embellishments to liven it up, but then it would be my show, not theirs. Somehow, I wanted my experience to have meaning for them.

"Later," I promised. "We'll talk about that later. I was on a jury and it was really interesting. But what about you? What's been going on?"

From the babble that finally subsided, I gathered that emotions were about evenly divided: they hated the sub; they thought he was terrific. They did work; they did not work at all. They gave him a hard time; they were very well behaved. Generally, they fared better than I (and I think, they themselves) had expected. I was glad.

After our catching-up talk, I asked them where they had left off in "The Scarlet Ibis."

"I'd like to get started with the story Mr. Lewis said you began—"

"What about your trial?" A protest from the front row.

"You'll hear about it soon. It's just that I need to get settled first into a routine, okay? Besides, this story, come to think of it, relates more or less to the whole idea of a trial. It's about responsibility for someone's life, and guilt about someone's death. James Hurst

15

is the author; he doesn't give us any answers, but he does raise some provocative questions."

Amy raised her hand.

"I have a question about that. I read this short story about a girl who finds her boyfriend with another woman. She's so upset that she runs out of his apartment, doesn't look where she's going, and gets hit by a car. Is that his fault?"

"I've seen that same plot on television. Do you think it's his fault?"

"Not legally, but I bet he'd feel guilty about it!" she answered.

"You can feel guilty about a lot of things that aren't your fault," Angela responded. "How about the woman he was with? Why isn't it her fault, too? Why shouldn't she feel guilty?"

"It depends on what you mean by *fault,*" Dean said. "Legal fault is different from whether you know in your heart you really did cause it."

"Have you read any stories with that plot, Dean?" I asked.

"Not a story, but it happened sort of like that with me and my brother. I was bugging him, daring him to catch me, and finally he started to chase me. He slipped and fell. I didn't *push* him or make him trip, but I guess it was my fault for starting the whole thing." He thought for a second. "But I don't know—my brother's really clumsy. . . ."

The class laughed.

"I know what you mean, though," Natalie turned to Dean. "You feel guilty, and maybe he would've tripped anyway, but who knows?"

Ricky added a new thought.

"Look," he said, "it's like this. When your time's up, it's up. It's a question of Fate, not fault. And the chick would've gotten hit by that car even if she hadn't seen that dude with another chick!"

The talk continued unabated, and a plan presented itself to me. They were raising questions that could be discussed after they read the story, but why not air them through the vehicle of a trial? I could share my recently acquired "expertise" on courtroom procedure—they wanted to hear that anyway—and this was just the opportunity I wanted to personalize the experience for them. The defendant would be the narrator, witnesses would be the characters in the story, we'd select a jury and others in the courtroom—why not? I didn't have time to plan anything through, but I felt this was a good time to share my idea with the kids.

"I think he'd be guilty!" Michael was saying.

"You sound as though you're deliberating on a case," I cut in. "Can you reach a verdict?"

"No," Michael shook his head. "This is more like an argument. We'd need to know the whole story, not just what one person says she heard."

"How'd you like to have the opportunity to reach a verdict about a person's guilt or innocence—to be on a jury?"

Everyone looked interested, expectant, as I'd hoped.

"Aren't we too young?" asked Marcia.

"For a real jury, yes," I agreed, "but we could have a trial right here is this room! I know how to do it now, and in "The Scarlet Ibis" there's enough material for a trial. You'll have to read it carefully, of course, tonight, and think about it; if you all agree, we'll start tomorrow!"

"I wanna be the judge!" announced Ricky.

"No, I'm going to be the judge," affirmed Mitchell. "No, I changed my mind. I want to be on trial."

"Good," said Donna. "I hope they hang you."

The class ended.

The next day we didn't discuss the story; the kids said that this case was not supposed to be discussed with anyone. Instead we made a list of everyone we'd need for the trial.

From the story we had James, the defendant, charged with manslaughter in the death of his young, crippled brother. James's mother, father, and aunt were witnesses, as would be the doctor who had attended the boy's birth and the medical examiner who certified his death.

We would need a judge, a bailiff, a court stenographer, two lawyers and their assistants, twelve jurors and two alternates.

This accounted for twenty-seven parts in our drama. We needed four more, and the entire class would be involved!

"Let them be character witnesses," someone suggested, and it was done.

Since every student was to have a role, no one hassled over any special one. A surprise volunteer was Danny, the boy who wanted to quit school, the boy who hated changes, who rarely spoke in class. He wanted to be the defense attorney, promising to win the case for Mitchell, the defendant, and grudgingly agreeing to take on David as his assistant. I had doubts as to his ability to carry out his promise. He'd have to read the story carefully, selecting facts pertinent to the case; he'd have to write his own questions and weigh the answers of the witnesses; he'd have to make quick decisions and pay careful attention to the prosecuting attorneys. I kept my doubts to myself.

Jeff and Matthew were the attorneys hoping for a conviction. Angela was the judge, Donna, the bailiff, and Michael, the court stenographer.

"Who wants to be on the jury?" I asked, underestimating the kids' mania for realism.

"Wait a minute," Danny spoke out indignantly. "Is that how it works? 'Who wants to be on the jury?' No! You told us you were asked questions—each lawyer asked you questions to see if you was right for the case, right?" He didn't wait for an answer. "Well, that's the way we should select this jury here. I don't want no prejudiced person on my jury!"

"What questions will you ask?" My doubts about Danny's abilities were diminishing.

"I'll have to think about them. Look, tonight, me and David'll get together and make a list of—what do they call that word—relevant—questions. Okay? And Jeff and Matthew can ask questions they think are relevant."

"Danny, that's a terrific idea. But I'd like to broaden it to include everyone. The more questions we get, the more interesting the selection process will be. If you reread the story tonight, you'll get a good idea of what lawyers would need to know to determine a juror's suitability."

"Could you give us an example?" requested Bruce. "I'm confused."

"Well, in one case I was on, the defendant was accused of stabbing a man who had cut him off while he was driving. So the lawyers asked us whether we had a license, how long we had driven, whether we had ever been angered by other drivers; questions dealing with the facts of the case. Of course, they asked for everyone's name and occupation. If someone had been a taxi driver, for example, one lawyer might want that person excused."

"Can we make up occupations?"

"Sure! It'll make things more interesting."

No one had any more questions, so I continued. "Danny used the word 'relevant.' What does it mean?"

"Having to do with the issue," Jeff responded.

"Good. I thought you'd know that. But there'll be other words whose meanings and spellings might be unfamiliar to you; you'll need to know them well for the trial. Let's write them down. You can get their definitions for homework."

The list grew as students recalled TV courtroom scenes. David Berkowitz's case was described daily in the papers during this time; someone had a morning edition and added "change of venue" to the list.

The next class began with Danny and Jeff collecting the questions everyone had written. While they discussed them, other students finished their definitions; still others moved the desks around to resemble a courtroom.

Soon we were ready. The bailiff instructed "All rise!" The judge entered and took her place at my desk. She banged her gavel; everyone laughed. She banged it again, looking stern.

"Order in the court: This court is now in session! Judge Angela Wearing presiding. No laughing!"

The lawyers began. Their questions were better than I had hoped.

"Do you have any brothers or sisters?"

"Have you ever resented their tagging along with you?"

"Are you afraid of lightning?"

"Would you stop to help someone even if it put your own life in jeopardy?"

Twenty-three prospective jurors were examined; fourteen were finally selected. The remaining nine snapped up the witness parts with no hard feelings.

At that point, Michael, our court stenographer, resigned, saying the task was overwhelming. He volunteered to be a court-appointed psychiatrist instead. I agreed, seeing an opportunity to get the entire class involved in writing.

"Keep a journal of the daily happenings," I said. "Write down what witnesses were called, what questions were asked—everything. Get old newspapers and read the accounts of the Patty Hearst trial if you need an example of what to do. It'll be interesting to compare your perceptions of the trial when it's over."

I realized it had been unrealistic to expect everyone to sit quietly and listen to the testimony all of the time. Keeping a journal would give the jurors and others a chance to occupy their hands and might decrease restlessness.

One day was allowed to prepare witnesses; the jury did library work.

The trial began.

Danny's opening statements were forceful and convincing. My doubts were completely gone now.

Jeff countered with an equally effective speech, and James

Hurst's moving little story came alive for us as it couldn't have before.

"Doodle" was born a hopeless cripple, doomed to die. His older brother James once tried to speed his death by attempting to smother him. But Doodle grew stronger, and James recognized his chance for a real brother, like the other boys had. Through a combination of love, infinite patience, and harassment, James taught his younger brother to walk.

But he didn't stop there. He pushed him without mercy to run, to swim, to climb; Doodle's handicaps embarrassed James.

One day, after a grueling workout, a violent thunderstorm caught the exhausted boys unaware. James ran for shelter, ignoring (or not hearing?) Doodle's cries to wait. Doodle, pushed beyond endurance, collapses and dies.

Danny contended that James had given Doodle a richer, fuller life than he would otherwise have had. He was fated to die, according to medical testimony, and James, who clearly loved his brother, could not be held responsible.

Jeff, on the other hand, contended that James was directly responsible for Doodle's death. Selfishness, not love, caused him to push Doodle far beyond anything his frail body could withstand.

Witnesses were called; prior testimony, in the form of the text, was read and reread. Objections were sustained and overruled. Recesses were called occasionally so lawyers could confer. Witnesses were recalled.

Finally, the trial was over. The jury filed out into the hall to deliberate. We busied ourselves while we waited.

Ten minutes later, a verdict.

"We find the defendant Not Guilty."

Everyone talked at once. Congratulations, hugs for Danny—it was almost as if he had been on trial. (And I think, in my mind, he was . . . .) The prosecuting attorneys wanted to appeal, blaming their witnesses for not being prepared well enough to withstand Danny. The bell rang during the clamor, Angela banged her gavel, and Court was adjourned.

We reviewed the procedure the next day and questioned the jury on its verdict.

"It was Danny who convinced me," said Amy. "He was so well prepared, he sounded so convincing, I had to let Mitchell off." The others agreed. "But also, the plot wasn't so realistic. He really didn't *kill* him. I think we should have had a different story," suggested Beth.

"Perhaps so," I agreed. "I also wondered how different it would've been if you jurors hadn't read the story first, but had to learn the facts just from the testimony."

"That's a better idea," several students agreed. "Only the lawyers should know the whole story beforehand. Can we do it again?"

I laughed. "Next year. For now, let's exchange journals. I'd like to see some, and I want you to see if your friends saw and heard the same things you did."

The kids pulled their chairs next to their friends, and I took a few minutes to go through the letters to me that had been accumulating all week. Danny's was on top: "This last week of the trial was really the best of the whole year. I guess it was the change of ways of doing things."

I looked up and caught his eye.

"Didn't I tell ya I could do it?" he asked.

"You certainly did," I nodded.

"I rest my case," said Danny.

Censorship:
Developing Language Performance

Raymond J. Rodrigues
University of Utah

Although English teachers feel a vague concern about censorship, few of us regularly engage in preventive action; rather, we wait until an attempt at censorship arises and then we react. Both NCTE and the American Library Association provide guidelines to help us ward off unwarranted censorship or, when censorship occurs, to help us respond effectively. Such guidelines wisely advise that, among other things, teachers be prepared to justify the selections in their curricula and that, as a preventive measure, teachers keep the public informed about and involved in the selection process, thereby enlisting the public as a potential ally. As a major classroom unit in senior high school, then, censorship study not only provides students with additional practice in evaluating literature and enables them to develop the language skills of listening, reading, writing, and speaking, but it can also lead to a more enlightened public, one which is aware of the moral issues involved in the selection of literature for classroom study. At the very least, students come to realize that literature does not exist in a vacuum called English Class but reflects community life, beliefs, and values.

A censorship unit such as the one described here can begin at any point in the curriculum but perhaps most profitably after students have started to develop their own evaluative criteria. A good starting point occurs immediately after students finish a controversial work that the teacher considers justifiable. Determining the particular selection should not pose a problem because certain titles repeatedly turn up on lists of censored works throughout the nation, such as "The Lottery," *1984*, and the ubiquitous *Catcher in the Rye*. (One caution: if referring to a specific work may cause some community members to demand censorship of it, revise the unit to focus on censorship in general, rather than on specific titles.)

To involve students directly with the moral issues in a given work, many teachers assign discussion activities and writing assignments that elicit specific responses to the literature. After considering those questions personally, students are ready to expand their orientation to the immediate community—their school, family, and town—and to the greater community—the nation and world. Perhaps they are ready to even ponder whether universal ethical principles actually exist.

At this point, the teacher can introduce the issue of censorship. Such an introduction may take the form of a hypothetical situation: "Suppose a group of people in this community demanded that we stop reading (*name the work*) in this school because they believe (*state a possible reaction, such as the work being considered obscene, too violent, too negative toward humanity*). Would they be right? Why or why not? How should the school respond? What do you imagine the community reaction to that response would be? Do you think the people in this community would actually react in such a way to this particular work? Did you?" Until this moment, much of the discussion will have been pure speculation, with students responding according to their own perceptions and experiences, but necessarily from limited data. Having established a basis for considering a particular work in terms of censorship issues, the teacher then selects from the following activities or assigns all of them.

Surveys. Consider with students examples of survey models, listing the examples on the board and including samples of the kinds of questions asked, designs employed for responses, and additional data collected about the respondents. Refer to concrete examples such as the Gallup reports. Suggest a number of ways to elicit responses, such as the semantic differential scale, a seven-point scale employing bipolar adjectives:

The violence in "The Lottery" is:

warranted   / / / / / / /   unwarranted

open-ended statements:

The violence in "The Lottery" is _____

or simple opinion choices:

"The Lottery" is too violent to be read in schools.

agree _____   disagree _____   no opinion _____

The class now decides the group they intend to survey—other students in the school, students in other schools, teachers, parents, or other community members. They also determine whether to interview people orally or whether to give people written questionnaires. Before they can determine the format for the survey questions and the questions themselves, students need to consider audience, purpose, and voice.

To create the survey, divide the class into groups, directing each group to develop questions to be asked in a survey about attitudes toward censorship, possibly about the censorship of a specific work. Then have each group present its questions to the class, with the class determining the most important questions, the format for responses, the number of questions to ask, and the means of collecting information about the respondents, such as age, sex, or other pertinent data.

Selected interviews. Assign students, individually or in groups, to find willing subjects for in-depth interviews about the issue, preferably subjects whose knowledge justifies the interview. Possible interviewees include other teachers, librarians, university professors, lawyers, and newspersons. Before the interviews, have students practice interviewing techniques by pairing off to interview each other about areas of personal interest or expertise. Another practice technique is to have individual students role-play famous people, living or dead, or characters from literature they have read at a "news conference" before the class of "reporters." After the interviews, the interviewers prepare written reports to be distributed among the class and kept for future class use.

Specialized research. Some students feel more comfortable reading for information than interviewing people. For them, assign the specialized research that requires only a few investigators. For instance, someone can find the address of the American Library Association and write that organization for its free publications. Later, the researcher reads and summarizes that material for the class. Another student can gather censorship information from back issues of *The English Journal.* A few others can search the *Reader's Guide to Periodical Literature* to find pertinent articles. These researchers, in turn, report their findings to other students whose task it is to prepare an annotated bibliography of available resources. This bibliography is then added to the class collection of censorship data.

Public meetings. If the class or individuals within the class believe that they should communicate their findings to the public, several formats are possible.

The *theater/forum* format requires members of the class or students in a drama class to perform a play that either addresses the censorship issue directly or that contains potentially censorable elements. The students themselves could adapt a short story, the drama teacher could suggest a play, or the class could find an appropriate play, such as Ibsen's *An Enemy of the People.* If the play is long, the director may choose to use excerpts only. Immediately after the public performance of the play, a panel of invited experts or concerned community members presents its response to the issues raised by the play, and the audience is invited to join in the discussion. For future use in English classes, students either audiotape or videotape the session. (Should the time to prepare such a play be prohibitive, many short films can be used to present a theater/forum.)

A second format is the radio or television *audience participation show.* Public television and radio provide opportunities for such presentations, and commercial stations are required by law to provide public service programming. The best "salesmen" in the class can approach these stations with a proposal from the class. If a station accepts the proposal, it will provide guidelines for the program. In its simplest version, the "guests" on these programs (in this case, selected students and/or individuals they invite) discuss their viewpoints and answer questions the public phones in.

A third format is simply that of a *panel discussion* before a public group, such as a school assembly or an evening session to which the public is invited. This format, however, is likely to be the least productive choice, and the motivation for audience involvement is limited.

Finally, students may elect a *videotape or slide-tape presentation.* If they do, any of the above formats can be employed, but "canning" the show has the advantage of permanence and carefully structured programming. Students revise until they are satisfied with the final product. By scheduling a discussion of the production after it has been viewed by an audience, students eliminate the negative aspect of no public interaction during the viewing. An additional advantage of this format is that it may be seen by widely spaced audiences.

Whatever format the class chooses, at the end of the unit they prepare a summation report, evaluating the total experience and making their own recommendations. The report is then presented to those audiences the class considers most relevant: a local English teachers' meeting, the board of education, the parents' association, community service groups, the school through its newspaper, or the town through its newspaper.

This unit on censorship has several advantages: it involves the class in a real-life issue; it compels students to employ a wide variety of language skills for divergent audiences and purposes; and it lays the groundwork for an educated school constituency, future parents who realize that controversial issues are an essential ingredient in literature study—if that literature is to have any meaning in our lives.

Using Student Questions to Promote Active Reading and Participation

Melvyn J. Haber
Pennsylvania State University

All of us have had embarrassing moments as classroom teachers. I want to describe one such moment because it clearly illustrates a problem I had with student passivity, a problem I think many teachers face. I have since found solutions to this problem, but I will tell you about them later.

The particular incident took place a number of years ago when I was a freshman English instructor. One day I assigned "Fern Hill," a rather difficult poem by Dylan Thomas, telling my students to come to class the next day prepared to discuss the poem. That night I designed a lesson plan containing numerous questions arranged developmentally. The first few questions were easy, but they were designed to elicit facts and concepts needed to answer later questions. These later questions built on each other so that by the time I got to my last questions students would "see the light," so to speak, and understand and appreciate the poem.

Much of what happened in class the next day reflected the difficulties I was having. As students came into the room and opened their texts, I noticed that, as usual, few of them had written anything in their books next to or anywhere near the poem. Class began, as it often did, with students depending on me to ask them questions. Those students who had not read the poem carefully, or at all, hoped that I would not call on them, while some of the others looked forward to answering my questions so they could get my praise for a right answer. As the discussion proceeded, therefore, only a small number of students participated. Fortunately, they came up with some good answers during the period.

It was, however, one of these good answers that led to the response that greatly embarrassed me. Shortly before the end of the period, I asked a question designed to put many parts of the poem together for the students to clarify its meaning. As soon as someone gave the answer, a bright, young woman called out, "Oh, that's where you've been leading us." She was right, of course. I had been manipulating the students to arrive at *my* understanding of the poem. They were, in effect, filling in the pieces of my puzzle in the rigid order I imposed. With a red face, I agreed with the student, smiling to indicate that this sort of directed questioning was, after all, a commonly accepted classroom practice.

From that time on I became less able to accept that sort of class discussion. I had become aware of just how active I was and just how passive my students were. In both their reading at home and their behavior in class, I had been encouraging them to rely on me to do their thinking for them. Specifically, many would skim through an assignment without reflecting on what they read. When I gave them questions to answer for homework, they read solely for the purpose of answering my questions. When they came to class, they sat and waited for me to ask my questions. Rarely did anyone have questions of his or her own. Rather, I was the one who was doing the careful reading, the formulating of questions at home, and the asking of those questions in class. I was the one who was doing most of the talking in class. When I thought about this, I realized that if and when any student of mine picks up a book in years to come, that student will probably not know what to do with it without having questions from me to think about.

It took some reading and a workshop or two before I was able to make changes both in what I expected of students and what I required of myself; but when I made these changes, I was able to get students to become more active readers at home and more vocal participants in class discussions. What I have done, in essence, is to place the burden of asking questions on my students.

This does not mean that I have stopped asking questions, for I still do. I ask them in class discussions at the start of a term because I hope that they will serve as models for students to emulate. I also ask questions throughout the term to make students more curious about certain issues and problems. And, finally, I ask questions to stimulate divergent thinking.

But, as I said before, I now place the burden for asking questions on the students. Since I know that this responsibility is both new and difficult for them, I offer as much help as I think they need.

First of all, to ease students into the process and to get them to read actively at home, I ask that they bring to class two copies of at least two assignment-related questions, ones to which they do not know the answer. If they have no such questions, they may bring in two ideas related to the material that they want to discuss with their classmates. I keep one copy of their questions, thus putting some pressure on them to do the work as well as enabling me to judge the sorts of questions they are asking. The other copy, of course, they keep with them in class. What is done with their questions in class depends on the students' need for structure.

If I think they require relatively little structure, I encourage them to ask spontaneously any of the questions they have written down. Whether I divide the class into small groups or whether I work with the whole class, I suggest that the discussion begin with a question from a volunteer. I add that the class should answer it as completely as they can before someone else brings up another question. A variation of this technique is to ask students to list on the board general topics that relate to their questions. Then I ask them to form small groups based on the topic they are interested in discussing.

Some students need more structure, as evidenced by their inability to handle this "free" discussion. In that case, either in small groups or in the class as a whole, I have one student collect the questions, dictate them to the group, and then ask them of the group one at a time, just as a teacher might. If they want, they can even decide on the order in which they will answer the questions. In this way, students copy down questions which resemble a conventional study-guide or lesson plan. That list of questions becomes the basis for the kind of organized lesson that makes many students feel secure.

After relying on these methods for a while, I try to achieve more spontaneous discussions. For example, I distribute reading material in class, let's say a poem, and ask students, either in small groups or in the class as a whole, to interpret what is being said. To help them do this, I suggest that as questions and ideas occur to them, they should feel free to bring them up. My role is primarily that of a silent observer. With practice, this method works well. After initial silences (everyone is afraid to go first) students come up with good questions and ideas on the spot. Eventually, I feel free to join discussions with my own questions and ideas.

Now, you may ask, what if the questions students raise are not as "good" as the ones teachers ask. My response is that we ought to teach students to ask "good" questions. I keep a list of the questions they bring in and write it on the board or on a ditto. Then I show them the difference between closed questions, which have only one answer, and open ones, which have more than one. Moreover, I emphasize values clarification, so that students learn to raise and discuss values questions that relate to the subject matter.

On the whole, my aim is to encourage students to write thoughtful questions, ones to which they really want an answer, whether they are closed or open, convergent or divergent. Relying on an inductive approach, I have even gotten students to draw up a list of questions which should be asked whenever they read, for example, certain genres of literature.

I know it is not easy to get people to do something to which they are unaccustomed, and teachers and students alike know the rules of the game. But I believe that different rules must be used, that students should begin to do the work that teachers have always done. I learned a great deal from preparing questions for every lesson; I am sure that students, too, learn much when we let them take on that responsibility. As Charles Weingartner ("Affiliate Notes and Quotes," *English Journal* 59 [September 1970] : 858) so eloquently put it:

> The student needs practice in a role that requires knowing what questions to ask rather than that of memorizing somebody else's answers to somebody else's questions. It is nothing less than incredible that we make no provision for learning how to ask questions in all curricula from kindergarten through graduate school. Mastery of concepts and skills such as these can produce individuals who are flexible, courageous, tolerant, and who, as a consequence, can deal fruitfully with change rather than be terrorized by it.

A Step Beyond Role Playing

Phyllis A. Sherwood
Raymond Walters College, University of Cincinnati

Walking into my freshman composition-literature course, one student, a young woman, turned to another, a young man, and said, "I still can't understand how you could be such a, a—oh, I can't think of the right word, but I *detest* you!"

"Why, Carol, what's the matter with you?" John asked.

"Oh, I like *you*, John," Carol responded; "I just don't like you as Gregors!"

This conversation was the result of what occurred after several days of studying Ibsen's *The Wild Duck*. I had tried a method I had not used before. My objectives were to get the whole class involved and to make students more aware of the complexity of many of Ibsen's characters. I also wanted students to discover relationships between what they read and their own lives. Although the method—role playing—is not new, I believe that the structure of the lesson is original enough to be worth sharing.

First of all, I had the students work in pairs so that everyone would be involved. I assigned partners rather than letting students choose their own because I wanted to pair quiet or shy students with more outgoing ones. Each pair of students was assigned one role as a character, as the author, and even as Mrs. Werle, who doesn't appear in the play. The "characters" were to be certain about their personalities and their motivations during every scene in the play. To clarify confusing points, pairs could consult with me as character to reader or as reader to reader.

For the second part of the assignment, each pair drew up a list of questions, at least one question for each of the other characters and for the author. By writing out these questions, students would not later feel as though I had put them on the spot. The questions could be those a reader might ask about the play or those a character might ask about another character. In addition, I asked them to include some questions that went beyond the scope of the play.

At the next class period, we were ready for role playing. Each pair wore character name tags so class members would have no difficulty identifying the characters they wanted to question. Members of each pair were to take turns answering questions, although they could occasionally collaborate. As it turned out, it was a beautiful spring day, so we went outside and sat in a circle in the grass behind the academic building. I don't know how much the atmosphere affected the students, but I do think it helped them enter into the fantasy world of Ibsen's play. In any case, by sitting in a circle the students could see each other's name tags.

I opened the session by asking the pair on my right to ask the first question. Then we would simply go around the circle, asking questions of a different character each time unless someone wanted to offer a follow-up question related to the previous question. At first, questions and answers were somewhat stilted. Students asked obvious, factual questions, eliciting responses that relied heavily on textual information. As they got into the spirit of role playing, however, they began to ask more probing questions and to interact in more personal ways. At one point, a thirty-eight-year-old student said, "Stop! Hedvig's answer to why she believed she was adopted—'I was naive'—isn't good enough. I can remember being fourteen and believing that I was adopted. I was sure I was an Indian princess (even though I looked just like my mother) and that I would be rescued one day by my exotic, wealthy parents. Doesn't anyone else remember feeling like that?"

Once this statement had been made, several other students shared memories of believing they had been adopted. These observations led to a discussion of Hedvig's interest in fire and the students' own experiences of playing with fire. The result was that students developed a very meaningful understanding of Hedvig.

When we returned to role playing, the class became more speculative. Student pairs stopped looking at their prepared questions and became more involved in the character they were portraying and in how that character perceived other characters. The first Mrs. Werle tried to gain support, but finally everyone saw through her "moral" self-righteousness. Mrs. Sorby had to win over many people before the class accepted her as a good person. Hailmar and Gregors tried to defend their actions and to justify their motives.

The two students who characterized Mr. Werle faced a unique problem. Several students were convinced that he was an evil man because they believed everything Gregors had said or implied about him. Even though "Mr. Werle" was able to get some of these skeptical students to waiver in this opinion, he could not convince all of the students that he was a good person. This situation led to a discussion of how people can and do misjudge others, how people feel when they are misjudged, and how hearsay evidence can be misleading. At this point, even the quietest students were involved in the discussion.

Near the end of the period the questions asked indicated that the students had gone beyond the limits of the play itself:

"What did you mean by the statement you made at the end of the play, Gregors? What did you do after the play ended?"

"Hailmar, what kind of life were you living five years after Hedvig died?"

"Are you still an alcoholic, Dr. Relling?"

"Mrs. Sorby, or I guess I should call you Mrs. Werle, how did your marriage work out?"

The answers to these questions showed insight into the characters. The students were living the play—hating and loving each other—frustrated, puzzled, enraged, enlightened. Students had become aware of the many facets of personality; characters could not be classified as simply good or bad. The characters had become real to the students as is evident by Carol's remark to John as Gregors the following day.

I have used many methods—lectures, class discussions, small group study sessions, oral reading—to teach *The Wild Duck*. None of these methods evoked the response from the total class that role playing did. Pairing the students and having them write out questions also helped to achieve my objectives. In addition, the essays these students later wrote were among the best I have ever received because their comments were probing and full of insight. Their papers reflected their increased knowledge about the characters and themselves.

Although I first used this method for a play, it has worked equally well for other types of literature. Preparations for role playing—each pair understanding its character and preparing questions—can take more than one day, and the role playing itself can extend for more than one day. Thus, the entire exercise can last from two to five or six days. If the cast of characters is small or the class large, students can be divided into groups of three. While the students are role playing, the teacher can act as monitor, making sure that each student gets a chance to ask and respond to questions. However, thorough preparation by the students before they begin role playing and the support they give each other by working in pairs are vital to the success of this method.

The Marriage of Literature and Technology: Does an Engineering Technologist Need Jonathan Swift?

Roberta Dixon Gates
Southern Technical Institute

Do engineering technology students need to watch *Antigone*, to listen to Frost reading his poems, to study the political philosophies of Machiavelli, or to read *Gulliver's Travels*? Yes, they do. So do chemistry students and forestry students and music students.

For eight quarters I taught western world literature at the University of Georgia to students majoring in the liberal arts. Since 1966, I have been associated with Southern Technical Institute, a four-year, degree-granting division of Georgia Institute of Technology, which offers baccalaureate degrees in Apparel-Textile, Electrical, Industrial, Civil, Architectural, and Mechanical Engineering Technology.

There is a difference in the response to literature from these two groups of students, and I have developed new ways of teaching Homer, Vergil, Dante, Chaucer, Shakespeare, Swift, Wordsworth, and Faulkner.

During the Summer and Fall Quarters, 1977, I initiated "marriage of literature and technology" projects in four Literature I and Literature II classes. Each student was responsible for a visually-oriented project which "married" literature and technology. We discussed obvious ideas, such as the architecture of the Globe Theatre or the kinds of windmills that Don Quixote might have seen. Each student had an individual conference with me within two weeks so that we could discuss the practicality of his or her project.

What kinds of projects were successful? What really drew students into literature as they explored technological influences? The impact of science fiction was most exciting. These reports, a natural for the engineering technologist, included introductions to H. G. Wells, Edgar Rice Burroughs, and Isaac Asimov, emphasizing space and time travel and inventions. Students were quick to point out that Swift, in Book III of *Gulliver*, as well as Poe and Mary Shelley were the obvious parents of science fiction, along with Marlowe and Goethe in their treatments of Faust. Kurt Vonnegut, the creator of the engineer-manager in *Player Piano*, became a real hero.

The poetry of Georgia's own Sidney Lanier inspired a look at the topographical maps of the last century to see how accurate Lanier's descriptions of the hills of Habersham and the marshes of Glynn had been.

Electrical engineering technology students became fascinated with the writings of the ancient Egyptians, the cave drawings, the Indian language, and symbol writing in general because they saw a connection with their own electrical symbolism. One student even brought a tape made by a Cherokee Indian reading poetry in his native language.

Presentations dealing with the history of bookmaking taught us all about paper, ink, book factories, bindings, problems of colored illustrations, and book costs. Our study of William Blake so fascinated one student that he did some excellent research on the technology of copper engravings, bringing in slides he made of unusual nineteenth-century illuminations.

A Jamaican student, a photography buff, reminded us of the importance of light to mankind, the discovery of artificial light, primitive man's conquering of darkness, man-made lamps from animal fat, and finally, the role natural and artificial light plays in photography. He read from Genesis: "Let there be light." Then he introduced translations from several Bibles. His work in portraiture made us aware that different types of lighting in photography—basic, butterfly, and rembrandt—have much in common with different translations in literature. His conclusion was a reading from "Black Genesis" by Stoney and Shelby.

The sixth chapter of Genesis inspired two students to investigate completely different technological aspects. A senior industrial student reported on Noah, who took 120 years to build the ark. New vocabulary words were *cubit*, *ark*, and *pitch*. Although there were 600–800 species on board, with a male and female of each kind, there were only eight people. Assuming each person had approximately 100 pairs of animals to feed, and that ten minutes were required to feed each pair, Noah and his family put in a tiring sixteen-hour day. Hopefully, the animals were in a state of semi-hibernation.

George Dickey, a marine architect, designed and built the

USS Oregon, using the ratio of length, width, and height of the ark, but reducing the size by one-seventh. Because of the *Oregon's* stability, it was the flagship of the American fleet. Building the ark today might well cause a cost overrun since analysis shows that the ark, which is eighty times the size of a 1,500-square-foot house, would cost $225,375.00.

An electrical student from Israel not only added authentic and firsthand information about the land of Noah, but he also noted that the dove has been replaced by the local scale radar and the satellite map.

We found many more instances in the Old Testament which challenged electrical engineering technology students. One explored the actual construction of the Ark of the Covenant. Made of acacia wood, or mimosa, it was plated in gold, 2½ cubits long (3'9"), 1½ cubits wide (2'3"), and 1½ cubits high (2'3"). The top was solid gold in the shape of a crown, with the wings of two cherubs forming the mercy seat. This ark was a form of communication between God and the Israelites; since death came to any who touched it, the ark was carried by two poles also plated in gold. Another student speculated that the ark could have been a capacitor able to store a charge. He build and demonstrated this effect for us.

At approximately the same time that the Hebrews were battling their enemies, the Greeks and Trojans were engaged in their famous and long-lasting battle. Reading from the beginning of the *Iliad*, a student introduced the idea of mechanical technology as it relates to the development of weapons. The wild ass catapult, the large crossbow—the ballista—and the javelin-throwing catapult made significant differences in fighting techniques. For instance, the torsional powered crossbow could throw a 65-pound rock 500 yards. The American Revolutionary cannon could throw a 30-pound ball 1,000 yards.

The Greeks did not spend all their time fighting. Shakespeare reminds us of the architecture of the Parthenon in *Pericles, Prince of Tyre*. A fire administration student found Shakespeare's description accurate, and so gained respect for the bard as a technical writer. From drawings this student enlarged, we learned about the traditional Greek temple form, the symmetrical design, the optical refinements, and the fact that there are no straight lines in the Parthenon.

One student read from the historians Plutarch and Anthemius of Tralles about the Roman attack on Syracuse in 212 B.C. Archimedes was supposed to have routed the Romans by burning their fleet with mirrors. Dr. Sakkas, in 1973, had 50 Greek sailors direct 50 bronze-painted mirrors toward a small rowboat. In two minutes the boat was in flames. The original Greek shields acted as mirrors, an early demonstration of the use of solar energy. This student said he had gained respect for the ancient writers since he saw they were accurate; now he had more regard for their stories and poetry.

The Roman aqueducts mentioned in the writings of the historians led one civil engineering technology student to research the twelve aqueducts built between 312 B.C. and A.D. 993. He told us about the location of water supplies, the problems of land acquisition, the kinds of equipment needed, and the difficulties with boundaries, financing, contractors, and tunneling techniques.

Another C. E. T. student began with the statement of a Greek general who recorded his respect for Roman roads because of their number, their quality, and the quick travel they made possible. He reported on the roads in Rome, Italy, and the Roman Empire, showing through charts how the roads were built and the foundations were constructed; he went on to compare those roads with modern roads. Vergil's complaint about not being able to get a decent night's sleep in Rome because of the thousands entering the city on the many new roads suddenly took on added meaning.

A student who had actually gone to Rome showed us a piece of the Coliseum he had retrieved from the ground. Reading from the *Natural History* of Pliny the Elder, "But it is now time to pass on to the marvels in building displayed by our own city," this student noted that the advent of new materials and new methods had stimulated and shaped the new theoretical approach. In this case the new material was Roman concrete, used for the first time during the second half of the first century A.D.

An unusual approach to a classic, *The Divine Comedy*, was presented by a fire science administration student. In the field of scientific management, he concluded, Dante would have been superb. Charts used for efficient staff division correlate interestingly with Dante's ideas of the right person in the right place.

The Renaissance period is rich in challenging literary figures, such as Don Quixote, who led us to discover more about the history of windmills. Windmills, which pumped water and milled grain at the beginning of their history, are now being used as an alternate energy source. In fact, there is now an electric-powered windmill which Don Q. would have a hard time fighting.

Some students studied Shakespeare's plays for the first time. Our class study of *Romeo and Juliet* led one student to explore the history and construction of forts. A second play, *As You Like It*, took place in Italy, where the textile industry became refined during the 1500s and 1600s. This inspired a textile student from Rhodesia to do a visually exciting project. She made a black outline of each costume described in this play and then filled them in with colored pieces of fabric to show the materials and textures used during that time in the theater. With this presentation, she gave a history of the textile industry through the mid-1600s.

An architectural engineering technology student made cut-away diagrams of the Globe Theater. A mechanical engineering student, whose major interest was metallurgy, researched the use of metals in the Shakespeare tragedies, particularly the knife and the sword.

Several hundred years after Shakespeare, another Englishman rose to prominence. Swift wrote *Gulliver's Travels* at the height of the Enlightenment, and it is a satire on the four aspects of man: political, physical, intellectual, and moral. Swift needed a way to express adventure, irony, satire, and tragedy in his book. He characterized Gulliver in a manner similar to the way math students solve equations in engineering, a project one student illustrated.

The Romantic poets led two students to meaningful technological research. One studied about Westminster Bridge, and its importance in Wordsworth's life. He found out all he could about that particular bridge, the city Wordsworth knew, and the nineteenth century technology of bridge building. Then he compared that bridge with the Brooklyn Bridge, which reminded us of Hart Crane and his poetry.

A water sanitation engineer returning to school lifted out this quote from Byron's *Don Juan*: "Till taught by pain—men really know not what good water's worth." The student then went on to sketch Byron's European trip, showing the prominent part water played in the poetry. Then he introduced a brief history of man's efforts to purify water for his own use, finding out, for instance, that the world is 97.2% water but that only .6% of this is fresh drinking water.

Dickens and his vivid descriptions of the factories of his time helped one of our industrial engineering technologists to see how far factory management has come in a hundred years.

A new word can start a student thinking. One student had never heard of the word "metamorphosis" when we began Kafka. This student went on to discuss the metamorphosis, the transformation, of the vacuum tube.

Modern literature helped some students see that *Foxfire* and what one learns from *Lord of the Flies* are not so far removed.

Neither are the concerns of Thoreau and the problems of industrial pollution. Thoreau's "Doctrine of Simplicity" should be required reading for all industrial engineering technologists. One student even called Edgar Allan Poe the industrial engineer of literature because his writings did not waste motion, squander effort, or offer unnecessary hypotheses.

Ralph Ellison's *Invisible Man* and James Baldwin's *Notes of a Native Son* were a black student's first introduction to black literature. He was a graduating senior, and for his presentation offered his own autobiography.

Wallace Stevens, lawyer, insurance executive, and poet, spoke to many students. From his "The Glass of Water":

> That the glass would melt in heat,
> That the water would freeze in cold,
> Shows that this object is merely a state,
> One of many, between two poles. So,
> In the metaphysical, there are these poles.

One student indeed showed that a complete solar home will not be so different from the glass, that the cycle can be complete within a domed habitat.

These, then, were some of the projects. Another quarter I may do more—or less. But students did have a positive reaction. Together the interface between technologist and humanist was strengthened by our working to show that both poles are necessary.

2 Getting Involved in Composing

Producing a Slide-Tape Presentation for a Public Audience

Alexandra R. Krapels
Consultant, Language Arts and Social Studies

Today's high school students are media consumers. In fact, many of them are gluttons of the media, especially of the visual media. They watch television at home and often at school. They go to movies on their own time and even on school time as part of a lesson. In some classes visual media have become as much a tool of education as textbooks have been for so many years. Using the media in the classroom has proven effective not only because they give variety to our teaching but also because they appeal to the students we now teach—the media consumers.

One unfortunate result of media consumption, however, has been the development of passive students. They have become accustomed to receiving, to ingesting whatever the screen offers. Unlike real food which provides fuel for future energy expenditure, the media meal is merely ingested and usually not converted into any form of energy, physical or mental. Is it possible to turn our media consumers into media producers?

A slide-tape presentation is probably the least expensive and easiest media project to produce, and certainly it is not a new assignment for an English class. The challenge, however, lies in choosing a topic that is based on the needs of the students' community, in discovering material that will be viewed not just by English classes, but by many different classes as well as by community groups. The benefits from such a choice are many. Students must learn to address different audiences and to engage in both primary and secondary research. In doing primary research, they often learn to conduct successful interviews. Also, the teacher is relieved of being both taskmaster and evaluator since the public audience becomes the most important evaluator. Other objectives accomplished by preparing a slide-tape presentation include, for example, distinguishing between writing that is to be read silently and writing that is to be read aloud and recognizing the importance of tone and pace in public speaking. These points are usually discussed and practiced in English class, but the slide-tape assignment, more than most assignments, makes them meaningful. From the teacher's viewpoint, the most important objective achieved by this assignment is that it is process- rather than product-oriented. Of course, the product is important, especially to the students, but the actual learning occurs while doing the assignment.

Producing a slide-tape presentation seems difficult; at least it seemed so to my students and to me when we began the project. We thought that a media production was something you watched, not something you did. But the project proved no more difficult than any other research project after we had broken it down into manageable steps. Moreover, it was more enjoyable for all of us than the traditional research paper because the students were sincerely committed to the project.

For ease of reading, I have outlined the steps of producing a slide-tape presentation according to the task that needs to be done, the process used to accomplish it, and the product or measurable results.

I. The entire class decides upon a topic for its slide-tape presentation.
   A. Process
      1. Either with the entire class or in groups of four or five, discuss the following questions:
         a) What problems exist in your community?
         b) What services are needed in your community?
         c) What community services do people need to be made aware of?
      2. Students should be given a few days to reach a final decision. Proponents for different topics may want to present their cases to the class, but the final topic should be a decision of the majority. Successful topics include: "The Cost of Vandalism in the School" and "How to Use a Voting Machine."
   B. Product: the entire class clearly and specifically states the topic, the intent or aim, and the intended audience. These statements should be displayed in the classroom throughout the project.
II. The class determines what specific subjects within the broad topic need to be researched and names a research deadline.
   A. Process: the class brainstorms while the teacher serves as discussion leader and recorder.

B. Product: each student is given a copy of the subjects to be researched. The deadline is posted in the classroom.

III. The class researches the subjects listed in Task II.

A. Process

1. Students initiate research by inviting a pertinent speaker to class. For example, if school vandalism is the topic, the Maintenance Director for the school system or the principal can be asked to speak on the topic. Students should have a fairly specific idea of questions to ask as a result of Step II. All students should take notes during this session. If possible, the teacher should tape this session for future reference.

2. The class should now break into groups of four or five. (Sometimes it is best if the teacher assigns members to the groups.) Each group must have a leader and a recorder and a list of subjects to research. Group leaders then assign tasks to each group member. Recorders provide the teacher with lists of who will do what in each group.

a) Some group members will need to conduct interviews in order to complete their assigned tasks, so groups should practice interviewing by phone and in person by role playing.

b) The teacher may need to help students involved in secondary research locate information because these materials are often not found in a library.

c) The teacher should act as observer and advisor to all groups during the research step.

B. Product: each student turns in to the teacher the results of his or her research. At the top of a sheet of notebook paper, the student writes the subject researched and below this heading a record of the findings. If the student has researched more than one subject, each subject is recorded separately. The student should be aware that this record will be on display in the classroom and that other students will use this material for reference. All research records are then placed in a single looseleaf binder, which is located in a central place in the classroom.

IV. The class determines the writing demands of the script for a slide-tape presentation including: length of the presentation (most are 15-25 minutes long); total number of slides needed (not all the slides are accompanied by script—usually 40-65 slides coincide with the script while the remaining 8-12 slides

occur at the beginning and the end with accompanying
music): length in seconds for each slide which accompanies
the script (most are shown for 7 to 11 seconds); writing
style, which is determined by the intended audience and by
the fact that the script will be read aloud.

A. Process

   1. The teacher distributes a worksheet which lists the following questions concerning a filmstrip students will study
as an example.

     a) How long was the entire filmstrip?

     b) How many slides were included in the entire
filmstrip?

     c) About how long was each slide shown?

     d) What can you say about the writing style of the
script? About how long were the sentences? Were
the sentences easy or difficult to understand? Could
you understand all the words used?

     e) What aspects of the pictures made this a good film-
strip? a bad filmstrip?

     f) What qualities of the speaker made him or her a good
choice for narrator? a bad choice?

   2. After the students have reviewed the worksheet, the
teacher shows a filmstrip for them to critique.

   3. Using the worksheets as a springboard for discussion,
the class makes its own decisions concerning its slide-
tape presentation. The worksheets are kept on file for
future use.

B. Product: the class lists its decisions concerning its presentation and posts this list in the classroom.

V. The class composes the introductory lines of the script and
outlines what will be included in the remainder of the script.

A. Process

   1. The entire class can compose the introductory lines (5-7),
or a group of three can compose them while the rest of
the class observes and critiques their work. During this
observation period the teacher can alternate members
of this small group so that more students can participate
in the initial composing process.

   2. Outlining the remainder of the script can also be accomplished by the entire class or by groups of four or five.
If groups are used, the whole class should later reach a

consensus based on the outlines submitted by each group. This consensus outline should be written on the board.

   B. Product

      1. A copy of the introduction is placed in the looseleaf binder along with the research from Step III.

      2. Each student makes his or her own copy of the outline for the rest of the script.

VI. Students compose the remainder of the script.

   A. Process

      1. Students work in groups of no more than three so that all are involved in the composing process. The teacher assigns a section or sections of the outline to each group and an approximate number of lines which the group may use to develop each section.

      2. After these lines have been composed and neatly recorded, groups exchange work. The work of each group should be critiqued by at least two other groups. Each group should revise its own work.

   B. Product: each group neatly records the final version of its lines and turns this in to the teacher, who makes a copy of all the lines for each student. One copy is placed in the looseleaf binder for public display.

VII. The class composes the final draft of the script.

   A. Process: the final draft may be written by the whole class or by groups of four or five. Each student must have a copy of the entire script. If groups are used, the entire class or an editorial board must later make final decisions concerning script revision. Students must be sure that the script is fluent, that it is not repetitious, and that it has the required number of spoken segments.

   B. Product: the final version of the script must be typed with a right margin of at least three inches. Several copies must be made. One is given to the teacher, and one is placed in the looseleaf binder.

VIII. The class designs visuals for the slide-tape presentation.

   A. Process

      1. The entire class should design the visuals for the introduction. A visual may be a photograph or a graphic, which may be hand-drawn or hand-lettered. Although most of the visuals should be photographs, graphics may be used for effect or when a photograph does not suffice.

Students may wish to reread their answers to question "e" on the worksheets they completed in Step IV. The teacher will have to remind the students that although their visuals may be dramatic, they must be relevant to the topic and realistic enough to be reproduced on film.
2. The remainder of the visuals will be designed by groups of four or five. One group is given the task of designing the visuals for the title and credit frames, of which there are usually four or five, and the one or two concluding frames. Each of the remaining groups is given a section of the script for which to design visuals.
3. Each group will present its designs to the entire class for critiquing.
B. Product: each group makes two copies of its designs for the visuals. The written descriptions of these designs are recorded in the wide right margins of the scripts typed during Step VII. One copy is again given to the teacher, and one copy is returned to the looseleaf binder.

IX.   The class selects the narrators for the script.
   A. Process
      1. At this point students may wish to reread their answers to question "f" on the Step IV worksheets. The entire class should decide which speech qualities are desirable and how many narrators are needed. The class should summarize these qualities on a rating sheet.
      2. Using the rating sheet, students and teacher should evaluate those who try out for narrator(s). Only the teacher should see these score sheets.
   B. Product: narrators are chosen for the slide-tape presentation according to the class evaluations.

X.   Students produce the slide-tape presentation.
   A. Process
      1. The following equipment is needed: tape recorder and blank tape, camera and slide film.
      2. The class and/or the teacher assign the following roles.
         a) Slide-tape director/editor to assist the teacher in overseeing the production
         b) Narrators (already designated)
         c) Artists to draw the graphics
         d) Photographer(s)
         e) Actors, if necessary
         f) Technicians to build sets, etc., if necessary

3. Some of the production activities may be accomplished during class time; however, the teacher may need to arrange release time for taping and photographing. Often it is best if all taping is done in one session.
B. Product: using a slide projector and a tape recorder, students show their slide-tape to other classes, teachers, and selected community groups.

The students' work on this project may be evaluated in several ways. Since the teacher was not the sole intended audience, he or she is not the only evaluator. Because the students have been so involved in the process of producing the slide-tape presentation, they should evaluate themselves. The teacher may prepare a questionnaire in which students assess their own performances and what they have learned from the project. Also valid is a critique of the presentation by another teacher, perhaps a social studies teacher. The students themselves can prepare evaluation sheets to be filled out by each viewer. In addition, the teacher can evaluate the products of each step by recording how completely students fulfilled their responsibilities.

When my students worked on this project, they were less concerned with what I thought of their work than with the reactions of those who would view the presentation. In fact, I became less the teacher, and they became less the students; they became their own teachers. Finally, my students had a better purpose for learning than just earning a grade or satisfying me. They wanted to reach a real audience. Media consumers had indeed become media producers who wanted to contribute something worthwhile to their community.

Reader's Theater Script Writing: A Strategy for Providing Motivation and Peer Feedback for Student Composition

Don Adrian Davidson
Evergreen (Colorado) Junior High School

Providing students with activities that motivate and provide immediate, relevant feedback for their writing is a difficult task. Effective
composition strategies are structured on the principle that composition is a means to an end, not the end itself. Few craftsmen
master a craft because they want to drive nails well, stitch a neat
suture, or prepare a brilliant brief. Instead, people want to create
finished products: snug homes, healthy patients, successful cases.
The best motivation occurs when people have the opportunity to
create a finished product that has value for them. The mastery of
fine details—nail holding or spelling—assumes importance only
when the value of the finished product warrants the craftsman's
concern. Creating, producing, and performing reader's theater
offer students the opportunity to attempt a worthwhile finished
product, and give them reason to attend to the fine details of
editing, revising, and proofreading.

Reader's theater can be described as the oral performance of a
prepared script by three to five seated readers who portray their
roles using vocal and facial expression. A performance of reader's
theater does not require script memorization, theatrical costuming,
elaborate sound effects and props, or theatrical lighting. Reader's
theater, therefore, lends itself to the classroom setting. The bibliography accompanying this article lists resources which offer
specific suggestions for writing and producing original reader's
theater.

The teacher may provide published scripts as models, but for
most classes this practice is unnecessary and may even inhibit
original writing. The teacher can read student-written scripts from
other classes and suggest that students use favorite television shows,
well-known fairy tales and books, or real-life situations as source
material.

Although the teacher's instructions to the students should avoid a single, directive solution, clear, detailed directions must be given. As the facilitator of the activity, the teacher should specify the following:

1. The form and final draft requirements of the script.
2. The dramatic elements—plot, conflict, and characterization—required for a successful script.
3. The number of class sessions that will be made available to prepare and rehearse the scripts.
4. The minimum and maximum number of minutes a performance may last.
5. The audience—but consultation with the class may be useful here.
6. The dates for the dress rehearsal, the final performance, and the collection of finished scripts.

How much time is given to the reader's theater activity depends largely upon the class. If students have had a good deal of experience writing in small groups and speaking before their peers, six class periods may be sufficient. If students do not have this background, more time will be required. The teacher whose students have had few small-group experiences will find the resources for organizing groups listed in the bibliography particularly helpful.

A six-day lesson plan for reader's theater can be arranged as follows:

Days One and Two: Students select their working groups, brainstorm within groups for script ideas, and prepare an initial draft of the script. It is important that all students serve as writers of the script so that each student can contribute his or her own composition strengths to the group's effort.

Day Three: Each group reads its initial draft of the script aloud, edits the rough spots, and begins practicing the final reading. The teacher may wish to spend time here working with each group to help polish its performance.

Day Four: The class meets for the dress rehearsal of each group's script and acts as critic and audience for each performance. For large classes, extra time may be needed so that each performance receives audience feedback.

Day Five: Each group polishes its reading, incorporating any changes indicated during the dress rehearsal.

Day Six: The reader's theater plays for a live, student audience. Almost any group of students can serve, as long as the price of admission, filling out a short critic's report of each performance, is paid. The form for the critic's report is flexible, and should be developed by the students of the composition class. Requiring the students to determine the kinds of feedback information they need and want helps them to become sensitive to the importance of audience and purpose in any form of composition.

On performance day the teacher collects the scripts. Final copies must be received before the performance because when students can no longer look forward to hearing the applause of their peers, all motivation to write is gone.

It should be noted that no attention has been given here to the oral skills needed to present reader's theater. There are two reasons why these skills have not been discussed. First, the primary objective of the activity is to provide an opportunity for students to create a finished writing product that has value for them. A secondary objective is to create a setting in which composition skills will be evaluated in a format recognized as relevant by students. While students do practice oral skills, these are a bonus for the composition student and not the principal objective. Further, students are quite capable of supplying accurate and useful criticism of the oral performances without intensive help from the teacher. They can tell performers when the dialogue cannot be heard, when it doesn't make sense, when it doesn't hold their interest. More importantly, peer comments are always couched in appropriate language and at a level which effects alterations in the script or the performance, a result not always achieved by an English teacher's comments.

Inasmuch as this activity as outlined here does not concentrate on oral skills, composition skills receive a complete workout. As students prepare the scripts, they encounter and solve problems that must be solved by any writer. Faced with the prospect of presenting a final performance, student writers must recognize and define their audience, identify an appealing but workable subject, and write and revise within the framework of a definite form, a reader's theater script.

Because the script is the result of a group effort, three important things happen that can aid the growth of the student writer. During the initial brainstorming for ideas, each member has the opportunity to have his or her ideas aired and incorporated into the script. Such a process helps the individual writer learn how to select topics, how to find supporting details, and how to eliminate extraneous material. Secondly, as the group works together, reading and re-reading its script aloud, individual students learn valuable editing techniques. Lastly, and perhaps the most important element in an individual's growth as a writer, each member of the group shares in the final success of the composition. If students are to become self-motivated writers, the composition class must provide opportunities for success.

In addition to motivation, reader's theater supplies student writers with timely peer feedback. If it is a need to write that inspires composition, it is the presence of critical feedback that produces *good* composition. When students write for an audience they deem important, they take greater pains to produce their best work. This is not the case when the source of feedback is seen as artificial or unimportant. For many students, the composition teacher is just such a source. When students write and perform for their peers, however, they write to an audience they understand and can anticipate, an audience whose approval matters, an audience who will respond to the work with immediate and meaningful criticism.

Reader's theater provides a setting in which students are motivated to display their best composing skills, to improve them, and to develop others. Moreover, the activity nearly runs itself—a welcome boon for the harried composition teacher. Composing reader's theater scripts teaches young writers to consider their audience as well as the problems of sequence, clarity, and detail. The activity makes clear the need for revision in the composing process and allows practical application of years of work on mechanics and neatness.

Reader's theater works because it is the student who is most responsible for the success of the activity, not the teacher. Things are learned *best* through hands-on experience. Why should composition be excluded? If your students are like mine, and I am certain they are, they have volumes of good writing inside of them that can be channeled into successful scripts, stories, or essays. As teachers of composition our most important task may be to discover valid reasons for writing, and then to stand aside and let students write.

References

Organizing Cooperative Groups

Johnson, David W., and Johnson, Roger T. *Learning Together and Alone.* Englewood Cliffs, New Jersey: Prentice-Hall, Inc., 1975.

Johnson, David W., and Johnson, Frank P. *Joining Together: Group Theory and Group Skills.* Englewood Cliffs, New Jersey: Prentice-Hall, Inc., 1975.

Moffett, James. *A Student-Centered Language Arts Curriculum, K-13: A Handbook for Teachers.* Boston: Houghton Mifflin Co., 1973.

Stanford, Gene. *Developing Effective Classroom Groups: A Practical Guide for Teachers.* New York: Hart Publishing Co., Inc., 1977.

Producing Reader's Theater

Coger, Leslie Irene. "Theater for Oral Interpreter." *Speech Teacher* (now *Communication Education*) 12 (1963): 322-30.

Coger, Leslie Irene, and White, Melvin R. *Reader's Theater Handbook.* Glenview, Ill.: Scott, Foresman & Co., 1967.

_____. *Reader's Theater Handbook, A Dramatic Approach to Literature.* Glenview, Ill.: Scott, Foresman & Co., 1973.

Henry, Mabel Wright. *Creative Experiences in Oral Language.* Champaign, Ill.: National Council of Teachers of English, 1967.

Lee, Charlotte. *Oral Interpretation.* Boston: Houghton Mifflin Co., 1971.

MacArthur, David E. "Reader's Theater: Variations on a Theme." *Speech Teacher* (now *Communication Education*) 13 (1964): 47-51.

McClay, Joanne Hawkins. *Reader's Theater: Toward a Grammar of Practice.* New York: Random House, 1972.

Sandifer, C.M. " From Print to Rehearsal: A Study of Principles for Adapting Literature to Reader's Theater." *Speech Teacher* (now *Communication Education*) 20 (1971): 115-20.

White, Melvin R. "The Current Scene and Reader's Theater." *Today's Speech* (now *Communication Quarterly*) 15 (1967): 22-23.

Writing an Episodic Novel

Al Yoder
Southside Virginia Community College

One of the firm beliefs of English instructors is that reading can improve writing and, conversely, that writing can improve reading ability. Presumably this is why English classes study both reading and writing and why many teachers ask students to model their own essays on those in assigned readings. The reading done in these classes is usually not limited to the expository essay. Fiction and poetry are also included and, seemingly, the same argument should pertain to them; namely, if students write fiction and poetry they will better understand those forms of literature. Professional writers themselves have recommended this procedure. In *The Second Common Reader*, Virginia Woolf observes, "Perhaps the quickest way to understand the elements of what a novelist is doing is not to read, but to write; to make your own experiment with the dangers and difficulties of words."

Teachers are, however, reluctant to assign creative writing, at least in general English courses. Of course, if the instructor is teaching a creative writing course or a general English course to a special section of advanced students, the reluctance is minimized. Otherwise, the teacher who simply asks his average students to write fiction is likely to be met with gasps of disbelief and loud declarations of inability. Nevertheless, there are exercises that are appealing and require little creative sophistication on the part of students. One of the best exercises of this sort is to have your students write a novel, an episodic novel. In this sort of novel a character is established who simply undergoes a number of different experiences over a period of time. As Robert Stanton explains in his *Introduction to Fiction*, "In an episodic novel, the plot is composed of separate episodes, each fairly complete in itself, linked chiefly by one or more recurrent characters."

If you find the idea of writing a novel shockingly ambitious, your students will find it even more so. Before outlining the procedure, let me explain the objectives of this exercise so you may, in turn, explain them to your students. Although this exercise might be employed in a creative writing class, it is fairly mechanical and might prove inhibiting rather than helpful to those who seriously want to become creative writers. The exercise is better employed in a traditional class of English composition, but you should make it very clear to your students that you are not turning the class into a creative writing class, that you are not trying to make novelists out of your students, and that you will not grade them on their creative ability, if you choose to grade them at all. After explaining what the exercise is not going to do, you may proceed with its real objectives, the first of which is to make students better readers. As Woolf explained, if students try to work with the elements of fiction (description, dialogue, narration, conflict, point of view), they will better appreciate them in their reading. The idea is to learn by doing. For example, students may not appreciate the difficulty of writing dialogue until they have accepted the challenge themselves. And even if they fail to create convincing dialogue, they will have learned in the attempt. The second broad objective is to make students better writers. Simply put, creative writing can improve expository writing. Whenever students attempt to express thoughts and feelings on paper they are practicing, and hopefully improving, their writing abilities. And, of course, the expository writer does employ many of the rhetorical devices of imaginative writing.

With these two objectives in mind, let me turn to the procedure. As I have said, in an episodic novel a character is established who then undergoes a series of experiences. The instructor may want to stipulate the experiences, each of which constitutes an individual writing assignment as well as a stage of the novel. What follows is a sample set of possibilities:

1. Invent and describe a character: physical characteristics, habits, likes, dislikes, traits. (characterization)

2. Provide your character with a history: What has his or her life been like up to now? Who were his or her parents? What sort of childhood did he or she have? What were his or her friends like? (background)

3. Describe where he or she lives. (setting)

4. Describe a typical day in the life of your character.

5. Your character is going to leave town; describe what led to this decision.

6. Just before leaving town, your character receives advice from someone; recreate this scene in dialogue.

7. The first day out of town your character meets someone strange; describe this person and what makes him or her strange.

8. This person asks your character to do something, but your character is not sure if he or she should. What was your character asked to do and what goes through his or her mind?

9. Your character decides to do what has been asked; describe the decision and its consequences.

10. Some time later, your character turns up in a large city with very little money. Your character decides to find a job. Describe the search for a job and the job he or she finally secures.

11. Describe a typical day on the job.

12. Despite the fact that your character likes the job, he or she is fired. Describe this scene, making clear why he or she was fired.

13. Your character is depressed and inattentive. As a result, he or she has an accident. Describe it.

14. Your character is taken to a hospital and learns that he or she is not expected to live. Describe this scene and your character's feelings about the imminence of death.

15. Despite the doctor's predictions, your character recovers and decides the city is not for him or her. Your character moves to a small town where he or she lives for a year. Describe this period.

16. While living in this small town, your character sees a number of things he or she believes ought to be changed. What are they?

17. In order to bring about changes in the town, your character decides to run for mayor. Describe the campaign.

18. Your character wins the campaign and begins to inaugurate changes; however, he or she encounters difficulties. What are they?

As you see, possibilities for this assignment are endless and can be organized around emotions—grief, shame, envy—as well as events. You might, of course, use some of the suggestions given above or devise your own, but a third, and very useful option is to ask your students to suggest assignments. Before you do this, however, you and the class must make a decision about the novels. Will they be serious or comic? This decision will affect the experiences that can be included. For example, an assignment might suggest that the character has had an accident; such an experience could happen to any character that anyone in the class is developing. Another suggestion—that the character gets drunk, for example—would not fit every character or would fit only comically, such as the intoxication of a puritanical schoolmarm. If you and the class have agreed that the novels are to be freewheeling and potentially comic, any sort of experience is permissible. If, however, you have decided to be more realistic and serious, then only very general suggestions appropriate to any sort of character can be considered.

Once you have decided on the general experiences that will comprise the assignments, the procedure is straightforward. Each experience or two becomes a writing assignment. At the beginning of each period, merely describe to the students the experience their character is to undergo. Although they write about this event in any manner they choose, encourage them to stretch themselves, to experiment, to attempt what they have not done before. Clearly, the experiences can be written about in a brief and perfunctory manner, but they may also be accepted as challenges.

Each student may work independently on his or her own novel over the entire period, or students may work cooperatively, either by working with the same set of characters or by exchanging novels for each assignment, thereby developing someone else's character. Whether you decide to develop the novels cooperatively or not, periodically set aside time for each student to share his or her work with others, either by reading it aloud to the class, or asking a classmate to do it.

As an inveterate reader of texts on creative writing, I know that many exercises have been designed to initiate students into the craft of creative writing, but I believe this exercise has four advantages many others lack. First of all, it is comprehensive. It provides a broad framework in which all the elements of fiction can be integrated. It is not fragmentary, nor does it rely on the piecing together of many separate writing exercises—setting, imagery, and the like. Because this technique is based on a general framework, it can be used with almost any text you may be using. For example, if the text is discussing dialogues you can ask students to emphasize dialogue in the next assignment; if you are discussing effective description, you can ask them to experiment with description in the next assignment. Second, the exercise produces a written product that evolves. As the episodic novel grows, students take greater pride in their work. They look back and discover that they have written a great many pages, and this sense of accomplishment encourages them to write even more. Although the accumulation of pages is not the objective of the exercise, it is undeniable that the more you do, the more you think you can do. A third advantage is that the assignment can be terminated at almost any time. Students may work on their novels as long as they seem to be enjoying themselves and benefiting from the experience. When students begin to lose interest and the benefits appear to be diminishing, you can simply ask them to write an ending. Finally, the relatively mechanical nature of the exercise is an advantage, for it removes much of the fear of creative writing. It is this fear that inhibits many students from attempting creative writing and many teachers from assigning it. Students are not asked to create from nothing; they are given a framework within which they can work.

The Interview: Combining Humanistic and Cognitive Values in the Teaching of Composition

Janet F. Cochran
Elon College

The increased emphasis on student literacy in recent years has brought teachers in all disciplines face to face with the knowledge that improvement and change are needed in the teaching of the language arts, and most especially in the teaching of composition. I have recently intensified my efforts to discover composition assignments which combine "humanistic" and "cognitive" values. One result is the interview assignment which I am about to describe. The fact that certain other needs are met by the assignment is pure good fortune, but I will mention those later on.

First a word about terminology. By "humanistic" I do not mean the often simplistic "make-'em-feel-good" type of exercises sometimes recommended for facilitating "self-expression"; nor do I have in mind what Ross Winterowd refers to as the "touchy-feely" approach—that of seeking to convert sensory experience directly into written expression. Instead, I want to suggest that teachers of composition have not paid sufficient attention to alienation within the classroom. It is by now a truism that students learn better in a situation in which they feel comfortable and recognize a sense of community—a situation in which they are acknowledged as individuals and have an opportunity to experience success. And yet factors such as population shifts, the reshuffling of public school attendance zones, and increasingly overcrowded classes at all instructional levels tend to discourage the development of these classroom characteristics.

I have been looking at ways to escape two of the common constraints of student writing, that of teacher-as-audience, and worse yet, the vague, unspecified audience that almost invariably invites shifting levels of diction and a muddled tone. It seems to me that the sense of audience can and should be made a *functional* aspect of student writing.

Instructions for the Interview Assignment

1. The teacher may wish to begin by noting that the apprehension felt by some students is both common and natural since the interview is a departure from conventional writing assignments. The class is asked to compose a list of questions appropriate for an initial interview. Students are encouraged to submit questions of a concrete nature ("What places have you lived in your life?") as well as those of a more abstract or theoretical nature ("Suppose you were offered complete financial support right now. What would you do with your life?").

2. Students are paired off at random by drawing matched numbers but are requested to change partners if they find themselves paired with a close friend or roommate. One of several different methods can be used to arrange the interviews, depending largely upon the instructional level. If the assignment is used in a junior or senior high school class, a specific date should be chosen for the first interviews. If it is used in a college class, partners should be allowed time at the end of the class meeting to set up a time and place outside of class for the first interviews. Since college students sometimes complain that hectic or conflicting schedules make out-of-class interviews difficult, they can, as an alternative, be dismissed to find a quiet place to conduct the interviews during the class hour.

3. During the initial interview, partners ask each other some or all of the questions on the list, plus any others that may occur to them. Students are encouraged to get to know their partners, to discover similarities and differences, and especially to be sensitive to any area in which the interviewee is particularly interested or about which he or she has strong feelings.

4. Each student compiles his or her notes from the first interview, studies them closely, and considers his or her overall impression of the interviewee. (Junior high teachers may wish to skip the remainder of #4 and also #5 as this portion of the assignment requires a level of sophistication that may be beyond their students.) The student then narrows the focus of the interview by determining the *dominant impres-*

sion gained from the initial interview (such as educational and/or career plans, special interest or hobby, or a more abstract concern such as strong convictions about religion, marriage/family, the need for independence). Based upon this narrower conception of the interview, each student then independently devises a second list of questions that will explore the area on which the paper will ultimately focus.

5. During the second interview, the procedure is much the same as it was during the first. Now, however, students are usually more at ease with each other and frequently discover that interviewees reveal more in responding to the second set of questions (which usually revolve around an area of great interest to them) than the interviewers had anticipated. Each student then examines his or her notes from the second interview, adding personal observations and insights.

6. Each student then writes a rough draft. The length of the paper may be specified by the teacher or left to the student's discretion. A time for the third and final meeting of partners is set.

7. At the third meeting, partners exchange papers and comment on both the form and content of their partner's paper. As interviewees they are urged to indicate particular strengths of the paper but also to note where they have been misunderstood. Partners should decide between them how they feel about having a paper read in class. *Both partners* should consent to the reading of a paper.

8. Each student then writes the final version of the paper and turns it in. The teacher and class may decide together about the number of papers to be read in class.

The interview assignment represents perhaps the closest kind of relationship between writer and reader, with the exception of the "journal" in which the writer writes for the self alone. The reality that the writer experiences and is concerned with communicating is not primarily his or her personal feelings (as is so often the case in student writing) but rather the external reality of the interviewee, who is, of course, also the reader or audience.

What does this assignment mean in terms of humanistic and cognitive values?

In terms of humanistic values, it begs the obvious to say that partners get to know each other rather well. What often happens, if I am to rely on student evaluations of the assignment and also my own observations, is that interview partners become good friends through the discovery of shared interests and a common experience. Another possibility, which may be as valuable to the student's maturity, is that he or she encounters someone from a very different background and with very different views.

If we look at cognitive results, we discover that aspects of the partnership interview clearly strengthen writing skills. Perhaps most important, the communication process, as it occurs in this context, involves a different kind of audience. Although the teacher-as-audience is inescapably present, the instructor is relegated to the background. In the teacher's place is not a vague, unspecified audience but a *known, limited* audience who provides periodic feedback and thereby serves as a kind of gauge of the writer's communicative ability. In addition (and this advantage was enthusiastically pointed out by a colleague who tried the assignment) the focusing stage of the interview requires students to narrow the subject or "find a thesis," a process with which many composition students have great difficulty.

In summary, interviewing partners develop what I have come to call a symbiotic relationship. The feelings of affiliation which frequently develop between partners facilitate the desire to help each other produce the best paper possible. In addition, there is an undeniable component of egocentrism which helps to produce desirable results; that is, the reader, who is also the subject of the interview, has a very personal stake in the paper and is therefore almost as anxious to ensure its success as is the writer. Thus the final sharing session, while dreaded by some students, is usually lengthy and thorough. There is, in truth, a relationship that is mutually beneficial to both partners.

Student comments about the assignment have been extremely interesting. A common theme is the initial apprehension over the interview relationship with (in some cases) a virtual stranger, as well as the actual writing of the paper. The consensus seems to be, however, that although the interview paper is considered to be the most difficult writing assignment in the course, it turns out to be the most rewarding. "When you see how everybody acts on the outside," wrote one rather shy boy, "it's nice to get in touch with the inner person and find out they have some really good ideas . . . and also see if they share your views or how they differ." A number of students noted that they liked having a student audience for a change and that they also liked *being* an audience because, as one expressed it, "Reading my partner's paper carefully and trying to help her showed me how someone else writes, and taught me some things to look out for in my own writing."

All the way up to college age, students are deeply interested in each other and concerned about the way they relate to their classmates. The interview assignment utilizes this interest and enables them to improve their writing skills at the same time.

Correspondence:
A Medium Rediscovered

Collett B. Dilworth, Jr.
East Carolina University

Pat Wilde
Independence (Missouri) Public Schools

"Who writes letters nowadays?" we asked our senior English students in Independence, Missouri, and Fayetteville, North Carolina. It was not a compelling question; they didn't know or care. After a pause, several admitted they wrote letters to acknowledge gifts. Such correspondence was an investment (no thank you letter, no more gifts) and a response to parental threat. Eventually, students allowed that businessmen, lawyers, and compulsive lovers also wrote letters. "Does anybody here write letters regularly? Do any of you maintain a relationship through correspondence?" Two or three fiancé(e)s raised their hands but lowered them quickly. Needless to say, as we introduced this correspondence project to our students we found that as far as letter writing was concerned they possessed a singular lack of zeal and understanding.

In outlining the procedures they would follow during the spring semester, we tried to energize their attitudes. We told them that by exchanging letters each week with a peer who lived about 1,000 miles away they would have a chance to develop a significant, possibly deep relationship, in a unique way. They were offered the following rationale:

> Such an arrangement affords both a handicap and an opportunity. You will be handicapped because several powerful means of communication will be unavailable; for example, there will be no chance for two correspondents to meet face to face, to have phone conversations, or to exchange pictures, audiotapes or videotapes. On the other hand, the limitations of writing can be turned to your advantage. Because you cannot exchange visual and auditory cues, you will have the opportunity to make your language work especially hard, especially profoundly for you.

> Although you are far away from your correspondent, you may
> get closer to his/her hopes, values, apprehensions, thoughts than
> if you were actually in his/her presence. You will find that writing
> to make yourself understood by a new, distant friend will force
> you to examine your own thoughts and feelings quite rigorously.
> You may well find that writing can be a powerful means of self-
> discovery.

They remained dubious, but they were willing to give it a try.

The procedures were relatively simple. To begin, Pat Wilde's
students at William Chrisman High School in Missouri and Mary
Wilmers' students at Terry Sanford High School in North Carolina composed letters of introduction. Students were encouraged
to be autobiographical and self-descriptive. Describing the first
episode that came to mind when they thought of their childhood
was suggested as a revealing ploy. The Independence students
each prepared a 3"x5" card that outlined the type of person with
whom they would like to correspond. Their letters and cards were
mailed in a packet to Fayetteville, where the students and their
teacher matched up correspondents. Then the Fayetteville introductory letters were personally addressed and mailed to Independence. After a seven-day hiatus there began a weekly exchange of
letters that occurred 13 times during the semester. Each Wednesday,
class time was provided for writing, but mailing was delayed until
Friday to accommodate the absent and the temporarily uninspired.
Postage for a packet of letters ranged from $1.50 to $2.00. Letters
normally arrived on Monday and always by Tuesday.

Students were assured that no one except their teachers and
their correspondents would read their letters without their permission. They were told that the authors of this study would read
their letters rather carefully with an eye to conducting some
research and that after school was out the letters would become
the property of the authors until the following September, when
all correspondence might be reclaimed. Naturally all mail was to
be saved, and each student maintained a folder of his or her correspondence in the classroom. Every effort was made to assure
students that short of plotting mass murder, they could write
whatever and however they wished.

There was one giant prohibition. Nothing but the written word
was to be exchanged until the end of the project—no pictures,
audiotapes, or phone calls. Exchange of home addresses was also
illegal. In the last two weeks, however, pictures, a box of revealing
artifacts from each school, and videotapes were exchanged. In the
videotapes each student had about 30 seconds to speak his or her

mind singly or in small groups. The idea was to provide a durable structure for the activity and then to turn the students loose and observe what happened.

What happened was beyond anyone's dreams. We immediately concluded that young people have an extremely high drive to communicate significantly, a drive which the normal functioning of an English class may tend to mask. In fact, the curriculum for the entire semester faded into a pale background for this single, obsessively pursued activity. School office personnel who handled the mail were besieged each Monday by students seeking to intercept their letters as soon as possible. Each week it got more difficult for one teacher, Mrs. Wilde, to read the letters and to note the patterns of developing relationships before Wednesday because the students got more and more adept at ferreting out where she had tried to secret herself.

The assurance we gave them about the privacy of their correspondence was forgotten after the first exchange, for they could not help but share with their classmates interesting parts of their letters and interesting aspects of their correspondents' personalities. Still they did respect earnest, private confidences offered in the letters and kept these to themselves. The fact that the letters were read, even studied, by their teachers and occasionally by other students did not seem to inhibit their writing, and most of them maintained a frank and revealing dialogue.

In sum, what happened was a communications explosion that provided students a unique opportunity to write with purpose and consideration and that provided us with a mother-lode of data about adolescence and about rhetorical relationships. What follows is an overview of the types of writing in which the sixty pairs of correspondents engaged during the semester and some findings about what personal correspondence is and how the medium seems to work best. No student is quoted more than once and all names have been changed.

In the opening few exchanges certain topics and issues were almost universally treated. Students opened the correspondence by outlining interests and hobbies (sports, the outdoors, music), by describing the makeup of their families, and by recounting personal histories. The most demanded and most offered information in the early letters was the correspondents' course schedules. Somehow the schedules provided essential insights to the students as they tried to get to know each other. Almost all the early letters repeated apologetic, self-deprecating concerns about the lack of neatness, the "poor grammar" and the possibility, indeed the certainty, that the letters they were writing would be boring. Being boring was obviously the most feared and despised condition that could result from a relationship. In the majority of the first exchanges, however, students made strong attempts to reach out to their writing partners and to seek and give assurances:

> I would like to know more about you. How many in your family? Do you have any hobbies? Do you enjoy playing any sports? If you have anything interesting to write (or maybe if it's not interesting) about—make sure and do!!

> Your thoughts were impressive. I appreciated knowing my own feelings aren't that unusual.

> I enjoyed reading your response to my first letter, and I apologize for the shallowness of the 2nd letter.

> I think you made a good start in your first letter! You certainly did better than I did.

After the fourth or fifth letters such groping disappeared as the students' confidence in the medium grew.

By searching for patterns useful in classifying the substance of the students' letters, we hoped to discover ways in which student ideas and rhetorical perspectives vary during extended correspondence. Some of our findings may give the classroom teacher an idea of what to expect.

The voice of the students' letters generally progressed from "I" to "you" to people and things outside themselves, showing a greater willingness not only to share superficial details but also thoughts and observations about a wide scope of personal concerns. Specific details were offered and questions asked within a limited time span: the near future (plans up to college), the present, the immediate past (high school), and the distant past (childhood). However, we discovered that students tend to prefer more profound discourse. They believe it is more stimulating to be informed of what writers have concluded as significant than to be informed only of what writers have seen or done. More than anything, the students want to know how their correspondents *feel* about things.

While students do treat extensively topics other than their own personalities (school, religion, abortion, drugs, dating conventions), discussion of such topics generally fails to elicit commensurate response unless it is approached subjectively. For example, a student who objectively discusses the beliefs and function of his or

her church is unlikely to elicit extended relevant comment in return. On the other hand, a student who generalizes about his or
her own religious beliefs and attitudes in relation to a church is
quite likely to receive a responding letter in the same vein.

Humor was also an important element in student letters, sometimes revealing a side of the writer even classmates may not have
known. Our students tended to favor outlandish exaggeration and
fantasy:

> In case you were wondering, Indonesian field hockey is a sport
> played between two ten man teams. The object is to shoot a cro-
> quet ball into the goalee of the other team. Either baseball bats or
> tennis raquets may be used in this endeavor. The sport had its
> origin in Malaysia during the German occupation of the 1930's. A
> slight variation of the game which is played around here, allows
> the offensive team to hit the ball into either end of the goalee. Of
> course, there is a great risk that in this variation the goalee will
> get upset and quit.

> I could just picture you sitting alone in a corner sobbing away
> while the rest of your class read their letters because you didn't
> get one from me. Can you ever forgive me?!? I know it's no excuse
> but it just slipped my mind what with the hurricane and all. Oh
> don't worry any, it wasn't half as bad as the fire, and the orphanage
> they're sending me to is really a nice place. The fire didn't last
> too long because the flood put it out before it could reach the
> basement where my step-father kept me locked with the polar
> bears, and I have a real nice box of ashes to remember everyone
> by.

The motivating force of the letters seemed to be to discover
what kind of person "you are" and "I am." Most of the students
were caught up in this motivating force and learned well from it.
Prior to the project their attitude was that letter writing was a
desiccated form of communication, a dialogue with all the vital
juices squeezed out. And it is true that some students experienced
a dreary phenomenon that came to be known as the "hi-bye
syndrome," characterized by the opening, "Hi. How are you? I'm
fine." and followed shortly by the closing, "Well, gotta go. Bye."
Naturally this phenomenon militated against fruitful correspondence. Nevertheless, the helpless fury such letters engendered indicated the students' growing understanding that letter writing
is a unique form of communication.

In short, correspondence makes it possible to develop a relationship solely through the articulation of thoughts and feelings, and
for that reason students found it liberating. They found them-

selves able to express thoughts and feelings without concern for the myriad complications and responsibilities that attend relationships carried on in physical proximity. So while they were denied the rich, multi-faceted interaction available to people in one another's presence, they were also exempted from the inhibitions, and they could be uniquely precise, open and bold. Our students seized this opportunity and found a taste for writing we hope will remain with them for a long time to come.

A Writing Week

Joseph B. Moore
Oxbow High School, Bradford, Vermont

Most English teachers complicate the teaching of writing. My suggestion is simple: let students write. Walk down your high school corridor and peek in the doors of the English classes. Are the students writing?

We teachers have convinced ourselves that writing is a serious and complex task. Unfortunately, too many students believe us. We begin with drills for pronoun reference, subject/verb agreement, verb consistency, active and passive voice, and vocabulary. By the time we allow students to write, and after we have forced them to read thousands of poorly written exercises, we have convinced them of the truth in the old cliché, "It's not what you say that matters, but how you say it." And then we wonder why students hate English. We have transformed what can be the most exciting class in high school into the most dull and hated class in a student's memory. English is a subject without a subject. It is an academic form waiting for the students to supply the human contact.

Each day I meet with five English classes, a total of 147 students. The weekly format I follow is similar in each of these five classes, but the content shifts with each class because I am working with different writers.

Monday

For the first ten minutes the class brainstorms for topics to write about. Students discuss and jot down topics which interest them. Each student then chooses one of these topics and writes notes or lists of information, ideas, feelings, or recollections related to that topic. When the student is convinced he knows enough about the topic, he begins the first draft. The paper may be primarily descriptive, narrative, persuasive, or any other nonfictional type.

71

Often the student isn't aware what "type" of paper he or she is writing. Subjects range from the description of a rat to the proposal that the school initiate a gymnastics program. Most students choose topics more easily after the second or third week. I require only that the student be interested in that topic.

As students individually develop their topics, I sit at my desk, choose mine, and write for at least five minutes. This tactic is important: I do not immediately walk around to help students who are "stuck," and they learn to rely upon themselves. More importantly, students see me as a writer, anxious to start my essay. Finally, my writing establishes a quiet atmosphere; no one wants to disturb me, or any other writer.

After five minutes I walk to a desk in the back of the room. Now students come back, individually and quietly, for assistance and suggestions. In addition, there are two desks in the rear corner for student-to-student conferences. No conference lasts more than three or four minutes, whether it is with me or with another student. The two desks for student conferences acknowledge to students that they can help one another. They also prevent chatter in the classroom by designating an area for discussion. When students aren't visiting me in the rear of the room, I write my first draft.

For Monday night's homework, students continue writing the first draft.

Tuesday

Students continue to write the first draft. I take attendance quietly. There is no discussion in this class, except the conferences in the rear of the room. For the first ten minutes of class, however, everyone writes. I remain at my desk and write, too. Again, when I move to a desk in the rear, students can see me, or one another, for help.

Now I help them, individually, to add ideas and details, to edit extraneous words, to shift the focus of the essay. Our aim is to complete the first draft by the end of Tuesday's class. If a student completes the first draft during Tuesday's class, he begins revising immediately.

Students can improve their essays without the teacher's direct help. I urge them to read their first drafts aloud and to make corrections on the paper as they read. I urge them to read their first draft to parents, brothers, sisters, friends—anyone who will listen.

I want the writer to have an audience. Students need to know that someone wants to read or listen to their writing, not just to correct it.

Tuesday night's homework: complete the revision and rewrite the first draft.

Wednesday

In Wednesday's class we sit in a circle—with thirty students, a *large* circle. We pass our papers around the circle and read. The quiet is broken by an occasional giggle. Usually one student looks at me with a pained expression which translates, "I can't read Leonard's writing." I nod and secretly acknowledge the dilemma, urging him to be patient. Again, the purpose of this class is to have someone other than the English teacher read the student's paper.

It is important that I pass my essay around with the others. It stresses my role as writer/editor, not teacher/grader. Also, students read more carefully and quietly. One week, when I had not written an essay, I walked around the circle. I discovered that the students kept looking up at me and away from their essays. I was an intrusive force, an extraneous moderator who was not participating but policing. The students rightfully resented my role because I was no longer sharing with them.

During Wednesday's class we read some papers completely. With others, depending on how much time we have, we revise introductory sentences, suggest new titles, rewrite last paragraphs, or underline words we like. The primary focus in this class is perceptive reading; our secondary aim is positive, specific comment.

Wednesday night's homework: Each student takes home another student's essay and writes a three-part evaluation of that essay for the student-writer.

The first part of the evaluation is a brief paragraph in which the evaluator responds as a reader, not as a substitute English teacher, and writes what he or she thought the point of the essay was, what the essay may have reminded him or her of, or what he or she found most interesting.

In the second part of the evaluation, the evaluator lists ten specific strengths of the essay. Sometimes this is difficult—especially for students who have never received back a paper from an English teacher who specified strengths. Here the student evaluator notes the use of a good word, a sentence which contains no extraneous words, a sentence which "shows," a catchy title, an effective transition, a snappy ending. These evaluations become more comprehensive as the course progresses. In the first weeks some students don't know what parallelism is or what makes an effective transition. And some still can't read Leonard's writing. This leads to the third part of the evaluation.

In this section the student evaluator makes two specific suggestions—only two. The rule of specificity can be broken only for one generalization: "Please write more neatly." Suggestions vary in complexity: some recommend the addition of a comma, and some recommend the revision of the final paragraph. In either case, the evaluator not only makes the suggestion, but writes out the suggested change. If I suggest a different lead sentence, I write one I think will work.

Thursday

In Thursday's class, students exchange and discuss the evaluations and essays. During this class I move from couple to couple, ask questions, listen to comments, and collect three essays which received positive responses. I make copies of these essays, with the permission of the writers, for Friday's class. After the discussions are completed, students begin revising that second draft.

Thursday and Friday night's homework: revise and rewrite the second draft. Often this third draft is significantly different from the first. It is common for the third draft to become a starting point for an essay in the following week.

At the conclusion of Thurdsay's class each student signs a paper listing his topic for that week. I take these lists home, type them up, and post them on the bulletin board in class on Friday. In one month, my students discover five hundred or more topics to write about. These lists eventually become our greatest resource.

Friday

Friday is our pow-wow. We sit in a circle to discuss copies of three student essays. However, for our first collaborative look at an essay I begin with one of mine. This policy is often embarrassing, but it serves an important purpose. First, students discover that I am a writer and, secondly, that I'm human. I explain that I dislike too much negative criticism and that I work better when I'm encouraged. I ask students to avoid phony commendations but to point out words, sentences, or paragraphs they like.

Usually a brave hand will sneak up and the student will say, "I liked the third paragraph." Everyone looks to the third paragraph.

"Does anyone else like the third paragraph? What's in there that you like?"

Slowly we get more specific. We pursue these strengths for ten minutes. Then for five minutes students offer suggestions for change.

In most of my classes I agree with about half of the student suggestions, and I make these changes right there on my rough draft. About one-fourth of the suggestions are possibilities, but I explain why I like it my way. The remaining one-fourth are suggestions which are inaccurate, and fellow students argue about them. I listen. Quickly my fifteen minutes pass. I distribute the next paper and for ten minutes we discuss specific strengths. Then we make suggestions for five minutes. We use the last fifteen minutes for the third paper.

During this class each student participates in the process of understanding and improving an essay. We try to avoid two things: phony praise and making the writer feel as if he or she is on trial. An occasional reminder about your own sensitivity is helpful.

Friday night's homework: complete the third draft.

During the writing classes on Monday and Tuesday, I encourage students to move their desks so they aren't facing one another. Some students enjoy facing the windows, some like facing the corner, and a few enjoy writing at the large "teacher's" desk.

The responsibility for the success of the class is shared between teacher and students. The teacher is not accountable for the work, the students are. If a student hasn't completed an evaluation, it's his or her responsibility to explain to the other student (who spent part of his previous night trying to help a fellow student). They learn together by relying upon one another. It is important for them to realize that one writer's attitude affects others in the class. The concept of shared responsibility also affects the teacher's evaluation methods.

Every student has a folder containing each draft of an essay and each evaluation. These are numbered consecutively and dated. I evaluate their work by taking home each student's folder every three weeks and scanning it quickly, noting quantity, then quality. If a student is missing a revision or an evaluation, his or her work is unsatisfactory. During this review I note students who are too severe on the evaluations and students who need more individual assistance. I write brief notes to each student about the work in his or her folder, noting strengths, one or two weaknesses, and whether I want that student to see me for extra help.

A student whose writing ability is poor but who completes every essay and evaluation deserves a high grade. The reason is simple: I can help that student become a better writer if he or she works hard. That is all I ask. I do not grade individual papers and do not read everything each student writes. I am not only unable but unwilling to perform such a service. Most writers do not have readers for all their writing, and they are not graded on daily quizzes and exercises.

It takes weeks to convince students that they are writers, and weeks to convince them that you are a writer. Simplify the teaching of writing: let your students write—and write with them.

Reversing the Revision "Blues"

Alice Glarden Brand
Rutgers, The State University

True, the class had discussed how *real* concerns generate powerful writing. The teacher had talked about the importance of writing from personal experience. "Don't reject any idea," the teacher had cautioned. (That can come later.) "First get it all down." Well, the period ended before the teacher had made a case for revision, and the students had followed their instructor's words—literally.

One hundred and nineteen compositions. Some made little sense; others were witty, vivacious, even grievously honest. Yet students had been able to intuit the motifs that constitute an engaging story: natural or personal disaster, violence, subversive humor. Most important, no student was unable to identify a personal experience to develop.

But that's where the composition process stopped. Some students can't revise, others won't unless forced. Even those who are willing don't know what to do next, except for a perfunctory neatening of their papers.

In a campaign against the revision "blues," the teacher plans a series of activities to overcome the resistance to rewriting by equipping students with specific revising strategies. First, the teacher examines student papers for sentences, paragraphs, and whole stories whose array of flaws is offset by the potential of their ideas. To safeguard student anonymity, the teacher recopies the writings *verbatim et literatum* onto transparencies.

Phase I

The teacher opens with a brief, purpose-setting statement: "We are going to be looking at some of your first writings. At first I may be doing too much of the talking; however, before long you'll be doing more talking and more writing. And it will be through discus-

sion and writing that we'll learn, me included." The teacher flashes
on the screen a sequence of sentences, such as:

> My room, I share it with my sister.
>
> Paul is a husband and father of 3.
>
> As the train went around the corner it speeded up so fast that
> train seemed as it would fly right of the train tracks.

The teacher should affirm the inherent worth of the selections but
emphasize that teacher and class can together make them better.

The group identifies spelling errors, trims away obvious redun-
dancies, labors over a confusion in logic, and practices rudimentary
embedding. Most important, they've caught on. They are sparked
by the comfortable level of challenge and their success.

Phase II

Enthusiasm at this stage is fragile, so as students move to longer
(but not necessarily more complicated) passages, the teacher should
avoid dwelling on technical detail. There still remains a virtually
bottomless stockpile of ailments which the group is beginning to
tackle with almost sadistic glee:

> It was about in the summer and my brothers and I just got
> done finishing building a room down our cellar. The room
> was to keep snakes in.

The first repair efforts are astonishingly clumsy. Some students
resort to a chain of relative clauses. Others try consolidations that
cost them significant details. But the group continues to propose a
variety of structures until intention and syntax match.

This next example invites a different kind of scrutiny:

> There were many exciting days in my life, but one which has
> left a mark on my life is my first dog.

The teacher graphically (but playfully) demonstrates on Risa's arm
the kind of *mark* the dog in fact does not make, and a round of
rewarding "Ah's" is heard. And revising proceeds.

Almost a double crostic, this example provides an opportunity
for sports buffs to flex their syntactic muscles:

> At the six man, 4 people were left Mark, and 2 other people
> whose names are blurred and me.

The noise level increases as does the number of revisions collectively attempted by students for this, their most demanding passage thus far.

Some students experiment at the chalkboard. Others find that double spacing in notebooks provides them with syntactic elbow room. Finally, the original and the best reformulations are scrutinized side by side at the board.

Phase III

As the program proceeds, the teacher consciously avoids evaluation. Instead, the teacher circulates informally, monitoring progress through the quality of student participation and by perusing revisions students have jotted down in their notebooks. Students are growing relaxed; indeed, they are becoming engrossed.

The revising process goes on at every level: the word, the sentence, the paragraph, and the composition unit. As lower orders of writing begin to take care of themselves, students move to reorganizing at a more holistic level. The teacher alludes to the role of an editor to convey this change: "You will be looking at good stories. Let's say, ones headed for publication. But they need the finishing touches of an expert, and you're it." Attitudinal ground rules are reiterated: "The ideas are sound. You're concerned with the stories' making sense for your readers. Do they develop in ways that are clear and interesting? How much 'tampering' with an author's words can you, as editors, do before the original vocabulary and perhaps even the author's meaning are lost?"

The first story is flashed on the screen:

> The sun was beautiful, it was early summer. my best girlfriend who lives in New York. Owns 2 horses. This is the time of year to break in the horses. There was my favorite horse whos name was Silver Mist so I was allowed to break him in. Cindy my friend had her own horse. Silver Sunset. I guess that I didn't have the saddle on right and he started to buck and run widly. Well all of a sudden he came to a fence. He stopped short. The saddle slid down his neck to his had and I fell off. All that Cindy did was stand there and laugh. I got up and started to laugh too.

Students can identify the setting, characters, direction of causality, and comical climax. The teacher then plots onto a triangle the levels of narrative abstraction that move roughly from the general to the particular. With minimal prompting, students begin to sketch triangles and to fit events inside them. Further discussion leads to a refinement of the basic triangular pattern, that is, a two-paragraph breakdown that separates the general setting from the particulars of the episode (see Figure 1).

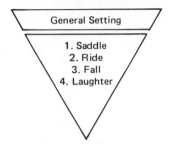

Fig. 1. Using a triangle diagram, teacher and class can plot the levels of narrative abstraction in a story.

In proceeding with this level of revision, the teacher encourages collaboration. Some students, with the oral impulse that accompanies adolescence, gravitate to neighbors. Others choose to work alone, seeming to rewrite from a series of mental trials. Whatever the arrangement, the noisy experimentation that accompanies the task is apt to reverse any impending apathy and to result in stylistic improvements. The efforts of two groups were viewed by the class via the opaque projector.

Stuart's group:

In the early summer I went to my friend, Cindy house in New York who has 2 horses. This is the time of year to break in the horses. My favorite horses' name was Silver Mist and I was allowed to break him in. Cindy had her own horse, Silver Sunset.

I don't think I had the saddle on right and the horse started to buck and go wild. All of sudden there was a fence and he stopped short. The saddle slid down his neck to his head and I fell off. Cindy just watched and laughed, I go up and laughed too.

Phyllis's group:

My best girlfriend, who lives in New York, ownes to horses. During the early part of the summer, I went to visit her and help her break in the horses.

My friend Cindy, has her own horse, named Silver Sunset. She let me break in my favoite one Silver Mist.

I guess I didn't have the saddle on tight enough, because as soon as I got on him, he started to buck and run widly. We came to a fence and he stopped short throwing me and the saddle on the ground. My friend and I started laughing as I got up from off of the ground.

The class agrees that Stuart's group has made a number of improvements. However, despite its questionable middle paragraph, the revision of Phyllis's group is soundly acclaimed as "better, easier to read." And the students can explain why. Dan and Lori point to some deletions; Philip and John notice variant word orders. By way of consolidating what they have learned, the group spends several moments trying out structural patterns for opening sentences, testing for themselves "what sounds right and makes most sense."

In order to concentrate on the progressive narrowing of narrative focus, the same story is again fitted to a triangular representation and its specific items of information are sorted sequentially. Motivated by the impulse to make sense of the action, students begin the sheer sport of the task, and end up with diagrams something like that shown in Figure 2.

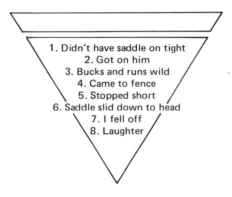

1. Didn't have saddle on tight
2. Got on him
3. Bucks and runs wild
4. Came to fence
5. Stopped short
6. Saddle slid down to head
7. I fell off
8. Laughter

Fig. 2. After another round of revisions, the triangular diagram can again be useful in showing the progressive narrowing of narrative focus.

This process enables students to compare systematically their revisions with the original (and coincidentally enables Phyllis's group to recognize that they incorrectly concluded that both saddle and author fell of the horse).

By now, the group is less and less intimidated by the written word. Some students are even willing to shed the protective shell of anonymity, and Lori has offered to hand out dittoed copies of her story:

> My room, I share it with my sister. She keeps the room in a complete "mess". So what I do is through her junk on her side of the room. She throughs a spoil little brat fit. I'm my sisters scapegoat about our room. If its a mess "Lori did it." Plus now I don't ignore her I just tease her.

> I hate being the middle child it's disguesting, I get in the middle
> of everything!!! When I'm fighting with my sister my brother
> picks on me and if I'm fighting with my brother my sister goes on
> his side. Maybe it will all change when I get older.

Students respond by exchanging personal horror stories for a bois-
terous fifteen minutes. Then, to get a head start on individual
reformulations, the entire class decides on some orthographic and
mechanical corrections and toys with one or two sentence consolidations. Regarding deletions, some argue that "spoil little brat fit"
is dispensable. The teacher polls the group. Many vote to retain
the expression but aren't sure why. The teacher prompts, "Does it
give you the picture you think Lori intends?" After some animated
debate, most agree it does. "Then, if it works for you, perhaps it
should stay," the teacher offers in an open-ended response.

Steve is more advanced in his revising skills than many in the
class and risks an almost complete paragraph inversion, reasoning
that "being a middle child is a bigger category than is being a
specific sister." Steve continues, "The story really has to do with
Lori and her sister in their particular bedroom." But, because
Steve "likes Lori's ending," he retains it in its original position. His
reformulation:

> I hate being the middle child. I get in the middle of everything.
> It is as if everyone is against me. When I'm fighting with my brother
> or sister the other one starts in.
> I share my room with my sister. She keeps the room in a big
> mess. So I throw her junk on her side of the room and when I do
> she throws a spoiled little brat fit. I am my little sister's scapegoat
> about our room. If its a mess "Lori did it." So now I don't ignore
> her I just tease her. I hope it will all change when I get older.

Though most students still make the more complex syntactic
alterations guardedly, they are at least not afraid to try. And for
virtually all students this activity has been a real eye-opener: a
hands-on experience in which they have become liberated from
the absolutism of the written word. At this point, depending on
student progress in performing these logical and linguistic manipu-
lations, the class may attempt more holistic revisions of increasingly
complex material, or may go on to rework a narrative in detail.

Observing the growing control over written language and the zeal
with which students are working, the teacher may select one last
story for revision by the class. Dan's autobiographical adventure
exemplifies the authenticity, the earnestness, the self-conscious
capacity of students to project themselves into a narrative.

> I remember one day two summers ago on my vacation with my family. We were at Cape Cod. So me and my little brother decided to go fishing. So we got our fishing equitment and walked to a peer. It was a rough day the waves were smacking against the shores. It was a long walk. When we got there we got out our equitment and started to fish into the roaring ocean. We were fishing anxiously until my brother yell and crying. I suddenly drop my rod in fright and ran over to him. I saw his finger got hooked by the hook. The sweat pouring down my forehead I tried to pull the hook out gently, but it didn't. So as easily as possible I yanked it out and we got our equitment and started to walk home. My brother wasn't crying any more. When we got home my family was out so I though and then soaked it in hot soapy water. Then I went out to put my equitment in the house when I notice my tackle box was gone. I left it I said I told my brother and ran and ran in frieght but the long distance didn't stop me. And the sweat coming down my body like rain. But finally I got there and luckly the tackle box was sitting right where I left it. So I walked home.

Dan's piece is laden with errors and immaturities. But because it represents the potential intrinsic to student experience, the teacher adopts a tactic that will enable students to proceed more autonomously and to work more intimately. Students now work in pairs. Based on the techniques learned earlier as a group, partners exchange and respond to each other's revisions, sharing in (or, more aptly, wrestling with) the process until both writer and reader sense closure. In short, peer feedback obligates students to compose intelligibly and convincingly.

To summarize, this approach begins by encouraging the student's natural voice to flood the page and then endeavors to bring that voice under control. Situation-specific, the revision program squares with student needs, interests, and abilities. It is equally applicable to lower order language skills and more complicated orders of linguistic and logical detail and abstraction. It avoids the passivity of formal language instruction and is an appropriate accompaniment to free writing. Finally, these revision tactics tap personal intuition, win a lively response, and focus on writing as an organizing and integrative act.

An Exercise for the Day Papers Are Due

Roger Whitlock
University of Hawaii

The days on which papers are due are usually days lost to instruction. If you've made a reading assignment, most students will not have read it; they were up late the night before writing their papers. Some time ago I gave up the notion that on days like these we would move on to something new, and for a while I devoted the class hour to exploring the topic my students had just written on. But most students were still so caught up in their own words that they couldn't listen to what others had to say. As they sat in class, they were still thinking about what they had written the night before, still struggling to make it clear. In broad daylight, many did not know whether they had won or lost, whether their papers were good or bad. And some no longer cared. In general, they were unable to stand back from what they had just written.

A year ago, I came to the conclusion that the best thing I could do as a teacher on days papers came in was to help the paper-writers to put some distance between themselves and what they had just written—to stand back from it, to look at it, to put it into perspective. There are several things I now ask my students to do before they hand their papers in.

Usually I have them start off by finding, and marking with an asterisk, the paragraph in their paper that they like best and think is best. I then ask them to turn to the person next to them and read that paragraph aloud—the person with the longest hair goes first. This part of the exercise accomplishes several things. Like a push-up or two, it wakes everyone up, gets everyone into the classroom and the present moment. And all have a chance to share what they have written with someone other than the teacher and to get an immediate response to it. (It may be a week or longer before they get my response.) At the end of this part of the exercise, the class is much livelier than it was a few minutes before.

I then ask my students to take out a blank piece of paper. I tell them that I will ask them to write down a number of things about their papers. They will have a minute or two to answer each question or respond to each statement. They shouldn't think too much about their responses; "Write the first thing that comes to mind," I tell them. I make it clear that I won't read what they write until I have finished marking their papers and have recorded their grades— in short, that what they say will not influence or prejudice me in my evaluation of their work.

Here are some of the things I ask students about their papers. (I vary the list from time to time, dropping some items and adding others.)

1. What makes the paragraph you read to the person next to you *good*—better than any other in your paper?

2. What was the biggest problem you had in writing this paper? Describe it. Did you solve it? How? If you didn't, what happened?

3. If you had twenty-four more hours to work on your paper, what—if anything—would you do with it?

4. Tell me something you learned about ＿＿＿＿＿ (the title of the literary work they dealt with) in writing this paper.

5. Tell me something you learned but couldn't get into your paper.

6. Tell me something that surprised you as you wrote your paper.

7. Tell me something you learned about yourself as you wrote your paper.

8. Is there anything else you would like to tell me about the assignment or your paper?

9. What grade do you think your paper deserves?

10. What grade do you think your classmates would give it if they had to agree on a single grade?

11. What grade do you think I will give it?

How students respond is almost always illuminating and occasionally surprising. We sometimes forget, I think, what good judges of their own work students can be. They know what is good and what is bad, where their words are flowing and where they aren't.

Of course, they aren't always aware that they know, and one of the values of the exercise is that it helps them to become aware. It also gives them a chance to put the writing assignment behind them. When I asked a recent class to comment on the exercise, one student wrote: "I feel relieved to write down these things." Nearly everyone said something of that sort. One said: "The exercise is very helpful—it's like washing your hands after you've finished the job." Another concluded: "It's like observing your paper as if you weren't attached to it." Several students told me that it was *hard* to do the exercise. One said: "I'm trying to be perfectly honest in answering the questions, but sometimes I just feel uncomfortable. Maybe it's because the truth does hurt a little bit." But most students liked doing the exercise; as one student observed, "It gives me a chance to say the little things that I would not ordinarily tell a teacher."

Students do tell me things that they can't tell me in their papers—for example, that they put a lot of time and effort into their papers and they're afraid this may not show. In such cases, although by the time I read what they have written in the exercise I have already graded the paper produced by their effort, I can at least acknowledge that effort. Often, my comment on a paper will say the same thing the student said in the exercise, and I feel as if our minds have met. If my response to a paper is quite different from the writer's response, I know that we disagree and I can act on my knowledge—either by writing a note or by suggesting a conference. But, in general, students *are* very good judges of their own work.

Reading what a student has written about his or her work immediately after I have read the work itself is a kind of bonus for me. Having finished marking a paper, I can relax for a moment and read what the student thought about the work, where it was strong and where weak. I can find out what the student got out of doing the assignment. It's as if I were reading short letters from my students, postscripts to their papers. Usually I add a short, quick note of my own, letting the student know that I have heard what he or she has said. The students have fulfilled their obligation as students by writing the papers, and I have fulfilled mine as the teacher by judging what they have written. As I read and respond to their comments, I feel as if I am establishing contact with them as people again, making this exercise valuable and instructive not only on the day papers are due but also on the days that follow.

Field Trips to Engage the Language Arts

Laraine K. Hong
Ohio State University

A special occasion of the school year is a field trip to some center of interest such as the local historical or art museum. The buses arrive, teachers and parent-volunteers shepherd the students along to meet the official guide. There is an orderly tour through the exhibits, perhaps a picnic lunch out on the grass, then back on the buses to return to school. The trip has been a pleasant diversion for students, but their participation has been mainly passive. Students were told not to touch, not to talk; they were told to listen, to stay with the group, to hurry along.

Back in the classroom, students are given time to express their impressions, answering such questions as, "What did you see?" or "What did you like the most?" They are then typically assigned to write a paper on what they saw. The paper is handed in, and the field trip is complete.

There are, however, effective ways of making the field trip a more productive and involving experience. EPIC, an alternative teacher education program at Ohio State University, has been especially active in using field trips to generate all forms of the language arts. The preservice students in this program participate in the kinds of experiences that they will eventually use with children.

First of all, they choose to visit only those places which allow students to wander at their own pace, to take ample time to observe, and where talking and discussion are not disruptive. To illustrate the kind of experience these students may have, let's consider a field trip to the zoo.

Before the trip the teacher visits the zoo, noting its layout and areas of special interest. Using this information, a trip booklet to stimulate and guide observation is put together for each student.

Each page includes directions at the top and ample space below for writing and/or sketching. Some possible directions:

1. Find a section which especially interests you (birds, lions) and sketch the layout of the cages, indicating where different animals are located.

2. Spend some time observing one particular animal. Record what it does, how it looks, what your own feelings are.

3. Interview one of the zookeepers or caretakers. Some suggested questions you might ask: What do you do? What's the worst thing that ever happened to you here at the zoo?

4. Record the scientific names for common animals. Record names of animals you've never seen before. You can do some word study back in class.

5. Use this page for any other observations or thoughts you may have.

These booklets need not be elaborate. Dittoed sheets stapled together with a cover page is adequate.

Before leaving for the zoo, students receive their booklets and the teacher describes the kinds of things they can do while there. Students are told they may work togther if they wish; at the same time they are encouraged to record personal impressions and observations. Instead of trying to cover everything superficially, students are guided toward an in-depth experience in a few areas.

After the field trip comes the happy problem of what to do with all the impressions, ideas, and information that students have recorded in their booklets. One approach to planning used extensively by EPIC is to web out ideas for follow-up activities (see Figure 1). Each source of information can be extended into several areas of the language arts. For example, those students who became engrossed in observing a particular animal could share their recordings, do additional research, and create a bulletin board of drawings and written descriptions. Webbing, it should be stressed, is done by the teacher to map out as many options as possible for integrating the language arts and the content areas (science, math, social studies).

The starting point was a field trip, but rather than being only passive spectators at this event, students actively participated in gathering information and recording their feelings and ideas. Back in the classroom, the field trip became a truly meaningful stimulus to language and thought.

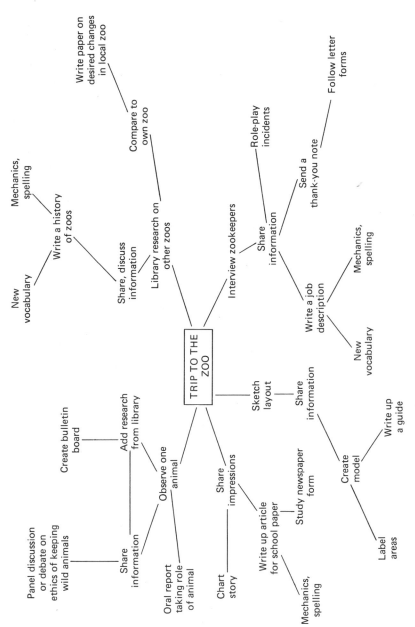

Fig. 1. Webbing the language arts possibilities from a field trip to the zoo.

Speech Communities in the Classroom

Karen Hodges
University of North Carolina at Charlotte

Perhaps the single most important characteristic of communication—oral or written—is sense of audience, an awareness that is emphasized in the rhetorical precept that undirected communication not only lacks focus but also fails to demonstrate that discourse is a process of interaction among speaker (or writer), subject, and audience. Any group of people brings together individual sets of language rules that have resulted from diverse factors such as cultural and ethnic background, years and types of schooling, and personal experiences with language. Because people seldom, if ever, stop to think about the rules of language they have assimilated—such as acknowledging an acquaintance with "How are you?" or establishing a certain physical distance from another person during casual conversation or maintaining (or not maintaining) eye contact—it is difficult for students to grasp that rules of language differ from community to community and from speaker to speaker. Thus when we wisely ask student writers to establish an audience for an essay, they may simply not have the knowledge to understand the audience's perspective, let alone select an appropriate style. To help students become more aware of these variations in language rules, I ask my introductory linguistics class not only to write language autobiographies but also to participate in a classroom exercise during which they divide into four speech communities, establish the rules of language for these communities, and then attempt to interact with one another. Because the majority of these students are preparing to teach, I am hopeful that this exercise will not only make them more sensitive to their own future classroom audiences but will also suggest to them a communication game that they can use to help *their* students experience the complicated nature of the communication process.

After the students have grouped themselves into four "communities," I tell them that they are to establish among themselves the language rules for their newly-formed communities, especially those considered appropriate for a social gathering at which they will meet "strangers" from another community. I also give them some general guidelines for consideration, stressing that they should bypass the rules of their own native communities:

1. What physical distance from another person is used for casual conversation? Is touching considered acceptable in speech community X?

2. What kinds of gestures, body action, eye contact should accompany speech?

3. What is the appropriate manner for addressing a stranger socially—Mr., Mrs., Miss, Ms.; Sir, Madam; first names; "Hey, buddy"; use of honorifics?

4. Is superficial "small talk" acceptable for establishing contact?

5. What topics are considered appropriate for a social gathering? What is taboo?

6. Does speech community X think it more acceptable to engage in ping-pong dialogue, to talk nonstop, or to listen attentively? Who initiates conversation?

7. Does speech community X make any distinctions between male and female language?

8. What level of style—formal or slang—is appropriate? What sort of intonational pattern(s)?

When each of the four groups has established itself as a community by means of agreed-upon language rules, I clear a space at the front of the room and bring together two of the communities to interact, reminding them that initial awkwardness is always a part of meeting strangers socially. The rest of the class watches the results, which never fail to be both funny and informative. It always seems to happen, for example, that speech community A has decided that aggressiveness is appropriate for social interaction while community B has opted for reticence. Not only does no real communication result in such a circumstance, but the students themselves find that they feel strange in either role and in the process discover that their own native communities obviously believe in some sort of middle ground between the two extremes. In fact,

one student whose classroom speech community endorsed personal closeness during conversation found she could not comply,
so ingrained was distancing in her own community.

After the "social gathering" dissipates, usually helped by uncon-
trollable laughter, the rest of the class suggests the rules that each
speech community must have been following; the participants
then explain how they felt trying to follow the rules. After this
discussion, the remaining two speech communities find themselves,
in turn, at a social gathering while the first two groups become the
spectator-analysts. The culmination of the exercise is a solid discussion of established rules in the students' own community, such
as the socially important though semantically empty "How are
you?" and the interesting rhythm of alternating speakers in con-
versations—most people even hesitate to answer a phone in mid-ring,
for example.

My rationale for this exercise was to bring home to students the
importance of sense of audience; to that I would simply add that
since language is a process, the teaching of language must, of
necessity, involve the students. To stand in front of a classroom
and lecture about how language rules vary from community to
community and about how the speaker-writer must adapt to
specific situations in order to communicate is to negate through
poor example the very nature of the subject matter.

3 Getting Involved in Poetry

Playing with Tools:
A Hands-On Approach to Poetry

Marilou Latocha
Morgan Park High School, Chicago

Enter a workshop. Carpenter Jones is making a small table. His tools surround him: a shiny saw bares its teeth at a hammer that remains undaunted, hard as nails. You watch fascinated as Jones picks up a tool to work. You listen to the singing of the saw, the steady growl of the plane. You breathe in the sawdust, are intoxicated by the varnish. You yearn to become one with the worker who is one with the wood. You long to pick up a tool, to join in the process. Just then Jones speaks. He reaches for something to give you. You hope it's a tool. But it's not. It's a list:

Carpentry Definitions

1. *Hammer* (n)—a tool with a steel head used for pounding
2. *Saw* (n)—a cutting tool edged with sharp teeth
3. *Nail* (n)—a tapered piece of metal used to fasten

Memorize definition and spelling of each word for test on Friday. You will also be asked to explicate a table, line by line, pointing out grain features and nail sizes. DO NOT TOUCH THE TOOLS!

And your love of tables tumbles.

"Do not touch the tools" is all too often how high school English teachers approach poetry. The tools of poetry are considered gifts of the Muse, too sacred to be touched by the grubby hands of adolescents. Teachers teach as their college teachers taught them, introducing long lists of definitions ("spell 'onomatopoeia' ") that are supposed to help students. Students, in turn, with eyes already glazed by years of passive TV viewing, find it easy to sit on their hands while the tools of poetry are "taught" to them.

Yet reading poetry is no less a skill than carpentry. The reader must "touch the tools." Mastery requires active participation.

The good reader is a creative one, picking up the poet's cues and creating the poem anew each time it is read. The reader, no less than the poet, needs hands-on practice with the tools of poetry. Explication is not a quasi-biological dissection—sticking in pins and labeling parts under a microscope. Rather, explication builds immediate poetic experiences through the actual manipulation of poetic devices.

Hands-on experiences, then, make up my basic approach to teaching poetry to high school freshmen. Before students open a poetry book, they actively experiment with similes, metaphors, and other devices through a series of exercises, both inherited and new. These include the following:

1. On the first day, I introduce a technique from Postman and Weingartner.[1] I ask students to take out a sheet of paper and write answers to fourteen questions, one answer to a line. The answers are not to be complete sentences but merely three-, four-, or five-word phrases; if students have no answer, they leave the line blank. Typical questions: Describe the odor of gasoline. How does hair feel? When the students are finished, I ask for volunteers to go to the board. Sometimes students write the answers to all their questions; other times several students each contribute one response. What results is a "poem," and we discuss its attributes.

2. Over the next several weeks, I hand out worksheets that require students to handle the following poetic tools:
   a. *Simile.* Really look at the room. Then complete the following: The surface of my desk is like _____. The chalkboard is as green as _____.
   b. *Metaphor*
      (1) Complete the following with the same word: She looks like a _____; she is a _____. (Emphasizes directness of metaphor.)
      (2) Metaphorical slang: Define each underlined term. How is it a metaphor? Is it a good metaphor?
         I be goin' to the <u>crib</u> when I see my <u>ol' lady</u> on the corner <u>rappin'</u> with this <u>bad dude</u> and sharin' a <u>square</u>. Man, I feel like <u>icin'</u> any dude be messin' with that <u>foxy</u> <u>chick</u>.
   c. *Denotation/connotation.* Cut out a picture of an old woman from a magazine or newspaper. Choose one of these captions: "She is elderly"; "She is old"; "She is a

senior citizen." Which is most complimentary? Why?

d. *Personification.* Act out "A Paper Clip Gets Bent Out of Shape." Tell what human attributes the actor kept. Write out the story using personification.

e. *Onomatopoeia.* Read a brief story aloud with other students, supplying appropriate live sound effects. Read the story again; this time students substitute word cards ("hum," "buzz") for live sounds by holding up cards at the appropriate times.

f. *Rhyme.* The teacher will begin a round-robin narrative poem by introducing a first line. A student will be asked to continue the story by adding a second line that rhymes with the first and so on. For example: Teacher: "Today I drove to school . . ." Student #1: "And I felt like a fool . . ." Student #2: " 'Cause I lost my cool . . ." Continue as long as possible. Discuss the difficulty and artificiality of rhymes.

g. *Alliteration.* Write alliterative sentences using these letters: z, s, t, l, k, b, p. For example: *Z*elda's *z*ebra visits *z*oos. How does each letter make you feel?

h. *Apostrophe.* Student actor talks to an object in the room. For example: "O desk, your scars tell of a battered life . . ." How do you feel doing this? Did you learn anything about the object?

i. *Juxtaposition.* Cut out words in large type from a newspaper or magazine and put them in a bag. Students will take turns going to the front of the room, picking out random words, and arranging them on a felt board. Why did this one go next to that one? Why did you leave this space? What does position do to meaning? To feeling?

j. *Rhythm*

   (1) Bring in a metronome. Read the following to its beat: (1) a school bulletin, (2) an item in today's newspaper, (3) a passage from a history text, (4) Kilmer's "Trees." Discuss the speech patterns heard.

   (2) Listen for five minutes to the natural rhythms of the silent classroom. List them.

   (3) Find the metric pattern of another student's name, for example: Robert Johnson—dactylic dimeter.

After about two weeks, I finally let the students open their poetry books. (By then, this action is thrilling, since it was so long forbidden!) We read poems and, as Ciardi puts it, see "how they mean":

> "What does the poem mean?" is too often a self-destroying approach to poetry. More useful is "How does a poem mean?" Why does it build itself into a form out of images, ideas, rhythms? How do these elements become the meaning? How are they inseparable from the meaning?[2]

I also encourage students to respond to poems we read by writing their own. But I don't force such writing, since many are still at the "playing with tools" stage and are not ready for real construction work.

Although these exercises are designed primarily for high school freshmen as an introduction to poetry, they can be adapted to other levels. For example, before they read Shakespeare, I ask students to experience his language by writing compositions using Renaissance vocabulary, for example: *Prithee, hast thou* seen my *bodkin* in *yonder* locker? Sonnet reading can be accompanied by "The World's Worst Love Sonnet Contest" in which students are asked to fill in the skeleton of an Elizabethan or Shakespearian sonnet (14 lines, each of which has only an end word that rhymes with the other end words in the prescribed pattern).

These exercises help to put poetry within the student's reach. Active participation increases learning, tempting me to twist MacLeish's poetic aphorism to state, "A poetry learner should do/ Not be."

Notes

1. Neil Postman and Charles Weingartner, *Teaching as a Subversive Activity* (New York: Dell Publishing Co., Inc., 1969), pp. 175-77.

2. John Ciardi, *How Does a Poem Mean?* (Cambridge, Mass.: Riverside Press, 1959), pp. 667-80.

Real Reading of Poetry

George T. Karnezis
St. John Fisher College

Anyone who has taught introductory literature courses realizes the special difficulties of teaching poetry. As teachers we understand that poetic language demands and rewards close reading. Since our education has made habitual a scrupulous attention to words, we are distressed when we encounter student resistance to the kind of concentrated reading we know poetry requires. Although we use various tactics to overcome such resistance, many of our students are left with the idea that close reading is a talent possessed by only the gifted. We need to involve students in "real reading" so that it becomes an activity that they, not just their teachers, perform.

To that end, I have invented a game which, if well played, helps students understand poetic language from the inside out. It puts them in the role of a poet; it forces them to concentrate on language as real readers should. The game begins with two versions of a well-known poem.

I

Every branch covered with it,
    Bent every twig with it;
Every fork like a white web foot;
Every street and pavement whitened soot;
Some flakes are wind-blown, and go upward,
Meeting those meandering down they turn and descend again.
    The palings are glued together like a wall,
    And there is no shape of wind in the fleecy fall.

    A sparrow enters the tree,
    Whereon immediately
A snow-lump thrice his own slight size
Descends on him and showers his head and eyes,
    And overturns him,
    And near buries him,
And lights on a nether twig, when its brush
Starts off a volley of other lodging snow with a rush.

The steps are a blanched slope,
Up which, with great despair,
A black cat staggers, wide-eyed and thin;
    And we take him in out of the cold air.

II

Every branch big with it,
    Bent every twig with it;
Every fork an angle of white;
Every street and pavement mute:
Some flakes have lost their way, and grope back upward, when
Meeting those meandering down they turn and descend again.
    The palings are joined together like a wall,
    And there is no waft of wind with the fleecy fall.

    A sparrow perches in the tree,
        Whereon immediately
A piece of snow three times as big as he
Descends on him and showers his head and eyes
        And overturns him,
        And near inurns him,
    And lights on a nether twig, whose pressure
Starts off a volley of other lodging lumps with a rush.

    The steps are a blanched slope,
        Up which with feeble hope
A black cat comes, wide-eyed and thin;
        And we take him in.

Neither version is the original. Both contain my variations in wording. Students are then asked to create a third and final version of the poem based on the options presented in these two versions. Wherever they find variations, they are to select what to them seems the appropriate wording. I use the following form so they can test out and record their decisions.

III

Every branch _____
    Bent every twig with it;
Every fork _____
Every street and pavement _____
Some flakes _____
Meeting those meandering down they turn and descend again.
    The palings are _____ together like a wall,
    And there is no _____ of wind in the fleecy fall.

    A sparrow _____ the tree,
        Whereon immediately
A _____
Descends on him and showers his head and eyes,

And overturns him
And near _____ him,
And lights on a nether twig, _____
Starts off a volley of other lodging _____ with a rush.

     The steps are a blanched slope
     Up which with _____
A black cat _____, wide-eyed and thin
     And we take him _____.

Several points must be emphasized if the game is to be properly played. First, since neither version is the original, there is no need to prefer one version over the other. Instead, choices are made freely from both. Second, the goal of the game is not so much to puzzle out the original version as it is to make a third version *based on justifiable choices*. The rules, therefore, require that each player explain and defend his or her decision as fully as possible. ("It sounds more poetic" is one common explanation. You obviously have to push the student beyond question begging.) Third, when the final version is complete, students ought to perceive that a holistic conception of the poem governed individual choices.

Clearly the best way of understanding the benefits of this game is to play it yourself. I urge you to do so before reading further so that what follows won't prejudice your estimation of the game.

I don't want to get detailed about the kind of play this game initiates, but I will offer some of my experiences with it. For instance, in the first line the choice is between "covered" and "big." Those who choose "big" do so because "covered" seems prosaic, even cliché. Discussion may follow about how poetic language struggles to avoid hackneyed perceptions. Thus "big" not only conveys the idea of coverage but also size or thickness. Further, "big" follows the alliteration of "branch" and "bent." For some, this may be the first time they become aware of alliteration. The sounds of words also become important when the rhyming of "big" with "twig" becomes a justification for the choice of "big."

Those who choose "covered" understand the justification for "big" but may still prefer their choice. Some find themselves unable to read "big with it" without thinking of pregnancy, as in "she was big with child." Certain students find such an association ridiculous, and a discussion of relevant and irrelevant associations or connotations ensues. Still others find the association useful and insist that, properly understood, it is an interesting metaphor: the snow seems not just to lie upon ("cover") the branches but gives the effect of having naturally expanded or grown—almost as if the snow were an integral part of the branches. Or, to put it another way, the branches were pregnant with snow. At this point, some may groan, become impatient, and complain of people "reading too much into" the poem. Their irritation provides an opportunity to talk about how to determine when a reader is reading "into" instead of "out of" a text. How can we tell whether the poet ever intended to trigger such associations? What criteria come into play when we try to answer such questions?

Once the game has gotten started, I find it valuable to remind students of the ways in which they're being forced to think about language. I urge them to listen to themselves playing the role of poet and reader. Now language seems less "on the page," more something solid to be formed and shaped according to their wishes and needs. To explain their decisions students find it necessary to talk about how factors such as context, sound, or rhythm dictated their choices. In so doing they gain a more comprehensive notion of what determines verbal meaning. Some students have confessed that the game made them, for the first time, appreciate what language (especially in poetry) can do. What they are realizing is that language is not merely a vehicle for delivering a message but, as Suzanne Langer and others have pointed out, a creative medium in which experience is formulated. Ideally, the game can develop students' perceptions of a nondiscursive use of language and lead them to appreciate what teachers mean by real reading: it is a matter of doing justice to a particular use of language so that the poet's "making" (which the game has brought into play for them) does not go unnoticed.

There are, of course, certain dangers in the game, the greatest being the risk of getting so bogged down in individual words or phrases that one forgets the poem's larger context. To avoid this, students must be pressed into the fullest explanations possible and reminded to look at the context. But dwelling on individual words or phrases is part of the real reading experience we want students to enact, and my own feeling is that it's worth the risk. As one student candidly put it, "Most of us read poetry the way we read the side of an orange juice can."

Another problem sometimes arises when you try to explain the overall purpose of the game. That purpose can truly be understood only through the playing. Initially, students may be disturbed when you tell them that the goal of the activity is *not* to "get the right answers" so that we can restore the poem to its original form. Whenever I'm pressed to tell what the original version was, I explain, without being coy, that it's been so long since I've seen it that I can't recall the original version. This move undercuts my role as "the person with the answer" and lets me be more of a player. I also hold open the possibility that we may, in our final version, make a better poem. The general idea is to put the entire class in the position of creators and not merely restorers of poems. More importantly, I want to emphasize the process, the actual playing of the game which, in a real sense, is its end. Knowing process is knowing how a poem means.

Demystifying Poetry

Andrea Friedman
University of Montana

The surest way to demystify poetry is to construct or reconstruct a poem for oneself. In fact, as Louise Rosenblatt points out in *Literature as Exploration*, any reading of a literary work is a reconstruction of that work in the mind of the reader. What is important here is the process of manipulating language, the composing process that the student engages in when confronted with a text. Students are encouraged to claim a poem as their own by using their own language to reorder the imaginative experience the poem generates in their minds. Thus, a poetry unit combines reading and writing. Both activities fall within the composing process.

What follows is a brief description of student-centered activities I've found effective in introductory poetry classes for secondary students. I am not suggesting that these activities *replace* the traditional approaches to poetry such as close textual analysis or a consideration of the chronological development of poetic genres and themes; I am suggesting that they should *precede* the traditional approaches. In some instances I've suggested ways of proceeding from an initial activity to more analytical and technical questions.

Starting Exercises

I find it best to avoid definitions, at least initially. Definitions, like emphasis on correct poetic forms, mystify the uninitiated and waste the time of those who already write poetry. In my starting exercises, I try to avoid questions like: What is a poem? What should I write about? Is this any good? These questions only increase debilitating self-consciousness. Instead, my starting exercises encourage anonymity, safety-in-numbers, reliance on someone else's words, and puzzle techniques.

1. Group Poem

Hand out strips of paper, one to each student. Announce the topic of the group poem and ask each student to jot down in four or five words the first image that comes to mind when he or she thinks of that topic. Collect the strips of paper and arrange them into a poem, neither adding nor omitting lines. Read the group poem aloud to the class with the topic as title. Hints: The topic should be something sensory, concrete, familiar. I usually use "Silver." "Sleep," "Fire," and "Water" might work well, too. Also, remember that it is going to take you five mintues to arrange the strips of paper into a poem, five minutes of dead time for the students. If noise bothers you, keep the students busy while you work. Finally, the "trick" to the success of this exercise is in the arrangement of the images and in the reading. *You have to make it sound like a poem.* I usually weave recurring words or themes in and out of the poem, and I make it sound as though one line implied its successor or predecessor even when I know each student had something different in mind. Lines that come out of left field can be placed either first or last. But the single most important factor is the manner in which you read these lines out loud. Read as if you were reading a published poem. Imitate the good poetry readers you've heard, especially those who read poems without strict iambic meter. Emphasize words for their sound value rather than for their meaning. Stress whatever alliteration, assonance, or rhythm you can find. If you do a good job of reading aloud, students will be amazed at their ability as a group. And every student will have had an equal part in that success.

2. Acrostic Poem

This exercise is especially good with younger children and with slow learners. Each student pairs up with another student and writes his or her name in upper-case letters down the left-hand margin of a sheet of paper, one letter to a line. That margin will become the base of a triangle of words lying on its side. Partners exchange papers, and each student writes a poem about his partner, using the upper-case letters at the margin for the first letter of each line. In order to make a puzzle out of the assignment, I use a numbering system that creates a triangular pattern on the page. The first and last lines must have two words (or syllables). The second and next-to-last lines must have four words (or syllables).

The third and third-from-last lines must have six words (or syllables). The triangular pattern can be achieved using either word-count or syllable-count as long as consistency is maintained. Example: My first name has six letters, so a poem about me would have the pattern 2—4—6—6—4—2 and might read:

> Acts like
> Nobody writes bad poems.
> Doesn't take much intelligence to see
> Right away what *her* game is:
> Entire world polluted with
> Amateur poets.

3. Cut-and-Paste Poem

This exercise can be done either in small groups or individually, depending on the size of your class and the resources available to you. For each student or each group you will need a pair of scissors, a jar of paste or glue, and a large piece of cardboard or heavy paper. Each student receives a copy of the same paragraph of descriptive prose (double-spaced). The student cannot add to or change any word in the paragraph, and he or she may leave out only up to x number of words (I decide the number beforehand). The student (or the group) must fashion a poem out of the paragraph. When everyone is finished, each person (or the spokesman for each group) holds up the poem and reads it to the class so that everyone can see it and hear it simultaneously. This exercise can be used with a creative writing class to begin an investigation of lining techniques in poetry. If further work is to be done on these poems, I have them typed up and copied for the class. The various arrangements will naturally lead to questions about how line length affects pace and rhythm, where the natural pauses occur in a typical English sentence, and how poetry plays syntactical pauses (commas, periods) against poetic pauses (line breaks) in order to create the syncopated rhythm we hear in poems. But for the general English class, I simply end the exercise with the sharing of poems unless specific questions are raised by students. Hint: The paragraph of descriptive prose that I use with my students in Montana is a description of the great falls of the Missouri River from the journals of Lewis and Clark. (I have modernized the spelling.) The students find the paragraph interesting because the descriptions are concrete and because most of them have seen the falls.

4. The Found Poem

A found poem is a poem made up of phrases or words that are picked up from (or found in) the environment. The delight people feel in reading a found poem results from the surprise of seeing familiar, content-oriented words isolated from their usual environment and arranged in a new setting which suggests a new meaning or emphasizes unusual sounds. It can be argued that this displacement of ordinary everyday words is the essence of poetry, the reason that poetry "begins in delight and ends in wisdom" as Robert Frost has written. A good found poem is arranged with some of the tricks used in forming the group poem. Give students specific ideas of where to look for words and phrases: newspaper headlines, magazine advertisements, cookbook recipes, owners' manuals, highway signs, signs around the school building. When the students share their found poems with each other, questions come up about the tricks of arrangement that make a poem out of ordinary, everyday words. After all, poets don't usually invent new words; they invent a new order. Here is a found poem from newspaper headlines:

February, 1977
President Carter Extends
Cold Front
Budget
From Schlesinger
To Drought.
Figures Unemployment
Buried Buffalo
Under 104 Inches
Of Congress.

The Poem in Sheep's Clothing

Another effective way of easing students painlessly into poetry without dealing with a priori limitations on poetry is to encourage them to write poems that are disguised as something else. For centuries the poem has played Proteus, assuming various guises as objects, letters, and other literary genres. I have used three variations of this technique.

1. Concrete Poem

The concrete poem takes the shape of the object it describes. I suggest that my students type them up. The idea is simple to convey if you have a few examples to show students. My favorite example is E. E. Cummings' dedication "TO" in his book *No Thanks*, which is also a found poem, consisting simply of the names of major publishing firms. It's a concrete poem because it's a toast (probably ironic, considering the name of the book) to these firms, whose names are arranged to form a goblet. A more complicated example is Cummings' "Grasshopper," in which the letters are jumbled in such a way that the eye moves over the page like the grasshopper moves in the poem. Other interesting examples can be found in the last chapter of *Western Wind: An Introduction to Poetry*, written by the poet John Frederick Nims.

2. Apology Poem

This is an idea that comes out of the appeal of William Carlos Williams' "This Is Just to Say." I usually hand out the poem and encourage free-wheeling discussion by asking if the students like the poem. Sometime during the discussion that follows, I ask whether they think Williams sounds 100 percent sorry that he ate the plums. We talk about things we've done that we've felt we ought to apologize for but deep inside we really weren't completely sorry that we did. Students then write their own "This Is Just to Say" poem about something they did or something they wish they'd done.

3. Letter Poem

I usually use Richard Hugo's letter poems, especially "Letter to Stafford from Polson" or "Letter to Logan from Milltown" because the area and concerns are familiar to my students in Missoula, Montana. The class breaks into groups of three or four. Each group composes a letter poem to someone everyone in the group knows. I usually make group poems available to the entire class, sometimes anonymously.

Getting More for Your Money

One of the major problems for the secondary school English teacher is generating several student-centered activities from one piece of literature. The problem is especially acute when the unit is a novel: How can I keep students involved in one book for three solid weeks? I don't believe in beating a poem to death, but I'd like to show that even a short poem can generate several activities.

Each of these activities may take several class sessions to work through. Although I don't recommend using all three activities suggested below with one class on one poem, I am presenting all three because I believe a teacher ought to be aware of the many possibilities a poem suggests and then choose wisely among them to fit a particular class. All three activities can be generated out of Theodore Roethke's short poem "My Papa's Waltz."

1. Poem Meets Short Story

Before I hand out copies of "My Papa's Waltz," I ask students to write in prose about the childhood they would have liked to have had. I specify that I want them to write in detail and to present that childhood as if it had really happened. I make it very clear to my students that I'm *not* asking them to criticize or defend the way they were raised; rather, I'm asking them to fantasize freely. I've found it helpful to let my Montana students know that my fantasized childhood involves a big white frame house with a porch that rings the entire house, a few horses, chickens, pet dogs and cats, and apple pies cooling on sun-drenched window sills. (I grew up in an eastern city, primarily in apartments.) The key to turning poems into short stories is to isolate the central question or situation of the poem (in this case, memory is turned into fantasy) and to present that question or situation as if it had really happened. Even a difficult poem has a common human situation behind it that can often be restated quite simply. Kenneth Koch uses this technique to teach famous poems to young children: If you could ask any animal any question, what animal would you talk to and what questions would you ask him? Koch asks the children before he teaches Blake's "The Tyger."

2. "Filming" Poems

The activity I find most successful with "My Papa's Waltz" (and with a few other poems) is to ask students how they would make a movie of this poem. We list on the board specifics for them to think about, such as: black and white or color? if color, what shades or tones would predominate? what does the set look like—props such as the kitchen table, sink, cupboards, floor, walls? camera angles? music? casting? costumes? lighting? special effects? I usually ask for answers orally because what is interesting about this poem is the variety of nostalgic scenes it elicits. Many of my students see a log cabin in the wilderness at the turn of the century. Others have suggested lower class farmhouses in England in the 1890s. Occasionally I get shabby frame houses in mining towns in the '30s. My own picture is of a city walk-up apartment of the late 1930s or early 1940s (possibly suggested by the movie *The Subject Was Roses*). Students enjoy hearing their classmates' movies, occasionally commenting on their choices, asking for more details or joining in to fill in what was left vague. They get the idea that reading a poem is a matter of getting a movie going in one's head. The trick is, as one student put it, to keep going back to the poem for clues about the set or camera angles until you have all the details down for your movie. There isn't one right answer although there *are* mistakes, like radios in turn-of-the-century log cabins. I find the "filming" technique is helpful in getting students into certain difficult poems. It helps them realize that they know quite a few things about the poem even if they can't give a coherent paraphrase of it.

3. Role Playing

I've combined "My Papa's Waltz" with other poems about parent-child relationships in order to role play a panel on "The Ideal Way to Raise Children." Students in the class can choose to be, for example, either Roethke's "papa" or "mother" or the child/speaker of the poem or the parent or child from one of the other poems. Sometimes I throw in a psychologist. Because there ought to be a moderator, sometimes I moderate and sometimes a student does. The rest of the class is the audience, and they can ask questions any time they want to (they must be recognized by the moderator first). I think I got the idea from "The David Susskind Show." Role playing is a bit scary for the teacher and the students the first time it's done, but I've had success with this activity as long as students remember to stay in their roles.

Voice Exercises

Approaching poetry through voice isn't new. I can remember an assignment I had to do as a college sophomore that required marking off the different voices in T. S. Eliot's "The Waste Land" and describing what the characteristics of each voice were and how one voice was related to another voice. In fact Ezra Pound and William Butler Yeats understood voice (or masks or *personae*) as a major structural component of poetry. I've used three voice activities in teaching poetry.

1. Masks

When you put on a mask, you become that creature; you speak from his insides outward. The animal can be revealed either through images ("My silver scales reflect all colors/as I leap from the water into the sun") or through image and sound ("I slither along without histrionics"). Students seem to enjoy becoming animals. I find this exercise especially rewarding when I require students to leave the name of the animal out of the poem. The class then guesses what animal is the subject of each student's poem.

2. Giving the Speaker Flesh

I choose a few poems—usually those with very different voices—in which the speaker has a definite voice. I ask the students to write a description of the speaker of each poem including, for example, age, sex, clothes style, hair style and color, facial expression, physical voice qualities (loud or soft, cracked, high-pitched, hesitant). I like using such poems as Ferlinghetti's "sometime during eternity," Stevens' "Final Soliloquy of the Interior Paramour" (a simple poem despite the title), Brooks' "We Real Cool," and Yeats' "He Wishes for the Cloths of Heaven." If the students seem to enjoy this activity, I expand it into a drama-writing or story-writing activity by setting up a meeting between two of the four speakers.

3. Giving the Mute Voice

I bring in five or six portraits, usually a mixture of paintings and professional photographs. I hand them around the room and let each student choose which portrait he wants to give voice to. Each student then writes a poem in which the person in the picture talks about himself or his life. Poems can be reproduced so the class can guess which portrait each poem gives voice to. Students should be encouraged to be specific about what clues they used to come to their conclusion.

Two Old Stand-Bys That Still Work

The first alternative is to play records and cassette tapes of poets reading their own poetry or of actors reading from the works of famous poets. Richard Burton's dramatic reading of Wilfred Owen's war poetry (Warner Bros.) seems to interest many high school students partly because of the bugle sounds between poems and partly because of the morbid concerns and violent images. Serious students of poetry in high school should be required to record themselves reading a poem of their choice at least once during the poetry unit. I find that I can get a fairly good sense of a student's level of understanding just by hearing him or her read. And the student learns a great deal about poetry—and about language— by trying to imitate Dylan Thomas' reading style.

The second alternative is to hand out a juicy poem or two and ask for reactions. Or ask the burning question the poem suggests. The juiciest poem I've worked with is William Stafford's "Traveling Through the Dark." Its question is: Did the speaker do the right thing? The chances are that after asking that question you won't be able to get a word in edgewise.

Involvement in the construction of poetry is the basis for any future act of criticism. Definitions, explanations, and critical opinions will otherwise not narrow the distance between the poem and the reader.

Teaching Poetry Actively

Laurence A. Becker
Artist in Schools, Bucks Harbor, Maine

"Your mission, should you decide to accept it, is to teach poetry to three tenth grade classes." Simple enough? But for the entire fall term? Thirteen weeks? While we're at it, what about having each student come to write poetry and even enjoy it? And as long as we've gone this far, why don't we go all the way and title our Fall Term English 10 course "Mission Impossible"?

Impossible as it may seem, just such an assignment has brought enormous satisfaction to students and teachers alike in the past several years. The two keys to the whole project have been the approach and the end product. First of all, there is no single assigned text; we use a shelf of forty to fifty poetry books along with a constantly growing collection of literary magazines from schools throughout the country, the Creative Arts issue of *Youth* magazine, the *Scholastic* Magazine Creative Writing Awards issues, and poetry folios made by students in previous years. Records, tapes, and films of poets presenting their poems are also available in the classroom and in the library. The approach is designed to enable individual students to begin a journey into poetry from wherever they are when they enter the course. An early assignment is to bring to class a poem the student likes. The poems discussed in class are the poems the students choose to present and the poems the teacher, as a member of the class, chooses to present. How to understand a poem—a critical method by which a poem is explored—is practiced daily in discussing the contributions of the class and teacher. If the critical method doesn't work with a particular poem (if the can-opener will not open the can), the method is examined and modified. Many poems are shared without critical comment because, as one person put it, "When you have to explain the joke, perhaps you told the wrong joke." The emphasis is placed upon sharing poems that class members have liked in the past as well as discovering new poems together.

The end product of the journey appears about two weeks before the end of the term in the form of individual poetry folios. The *only* requirement is that each folio contain poems in each of four different categories that demonstrate particular *relationships* to poetry:

1. *Something Old*: poems enjoyed before the course began. Some students may have had a few positive experiences with poetry, and they have few poems in this section.

2. *Something New*: poems experienced and enjoyed during the term. The variety here is indeed remarkable when students are given a chance to search and share.

3. *Something Borrowed*: poems that another person has shared directly with them. Of course, sharing is reciprocal, and giving goes along with receiving. Cooperation rather than competition is emphasized here.

4. *Something Original*: poems written by the student. During the term we meet many new poetic forms and try them out on our own.

The number of poems in each section is not stressed; instead, the emphasis is placed on the honesty of the student's response to individual poems.

Many students assemble hard-backed books and illustrate their poems with original art work or photography. These designs and materials embody a wide range of creative endeavor. The experience of sharing maintained throughout the term reaches its climax the day the folios are due. The sounds of delight, surprise, and even awe are evidence that the experience was indeed real and not just an impossible dream. Tenth grade students have read, shared, studied, written, memorized, and, above all, enjoyed poetry. The hope is that they will continue the journey into poetry.

Boggle Their Minds:
Activities for the Poetry Classroom

Robert A. Rennert
Findlay College

Many English teachers have heard poetry defined as "disciplined play," yet their teaching methods, either in literature courses or in creative writing sessions, tend to deny that definition. Traditional classroom activities, like lectures "about" poetry and quizzes that require students to memorize definitions of poetic devices, emphasize the discipline of poems and their formal qualities. Students frequently respond to such approaches by rejecting poetry as irrelevant and boring. On the other hand, a steady dose of activities like rhyming games can lead students to believe that poetry is essentially ephemeral and trivial. In neither case do the activities respond to the students' (and our) need for a balance of that freedom which permits creative experimentation and that discipline which is part of any art.

The following activities attempt to achieve the balance captured in the phrase "disciplined play." Although I experimented with them in a college classroom, similar experiences can be provided at many grade levels.

Boggle

Boggle is the Parker Brothers trademark for a hidden word game designed for play by two to six people (ages eight–adult). This inexpensive game is available at many department stores and consists of a small timer, a two-part plastic container, and a set of sixteen wooden cubes imprinted with various letters.

To begin the game, a player shakes the cubes inside the container until they settle in square slots in the container's base and form a random arrangement of letters. A typical array is shown in Figure 1.

The timer is now activated and players try to find words in the sequential vertical, horizontal, or diagonal arrangement. In the

Fig. 1. Boggle begins with a random sequence of letters which players rearrange verti-
cally, horizontally, or diagonally to form simple words.

sample above, students might find "was," "wasp," "pod," "peat,"
"dope," "buy," "bun," "fat," and so forth. At the end of the
time, players compare lists. Points are given only for words which
do not appear on the lists of other players. At the end of one
round, then, each player has a list of words he or she alone found
in the random arrangement of letters.

In a poetry class, the game can be used as a starting point for
creative writing activities. The very act of looking at combinations
of letters, testing their patterns, and discovering words is not only
exciting but also makes students more aware of how words are
formed, more aware of the richness of language that yields so
many words from so few letters. It also draws attention to the
qualities of specific words—the basic attention that any good poet
has developed extensively. Comparing lists also enlarges vocabularies
without the tediousness of "spelling lists." Finally, students frequently notice the similarities of sight and sound in the words
they find, similarities which, of course, poets frequently exploit.

Using the game as a starting point for a writing assignment helps
overcome student frustration. Often students complain that they
have nothing to write about. After several rounds of *Boggle*, however, each student has a stock of words that he or she alone has
found. I then ask them to begin with those words to compose a
poem. Frequently I do not specify the form of the poem, but if

we have been examining a particular form—like the haiku—I ask them to use that form.

In order to write the poem, students need to add appropriate words to connect the ones on their list, but what began as play, as a simple *Boggle* game, frequently evolves into a serious effort to find particular words and particular sounds. Students respond well to the experience of generating a unique resource (their very own list of words) and of using that resource to compose a poem.

Depending on the teacher's purpose, the game can be the prelude to a variety of activities—writing lines with a particular rhythm or sound pattern, illustrating a particular poetic device. In short, *Boggle* seems to generate enthusiasm for poetry.

Newspaper Syllabics

In traditional poetry lessons, students rarely experience the decisions a poet makes about matters like length of line and placement of words. A simple exercise like the one described here, however, helps students to understand and appreciate the craftsmanship of a poet like Marianne Moore as well as to enjoy playing with different possibilities for designing a poem.

I begin the class session by distributing to each student a page of a newspaper (the Sunday edition of a metropolitan paper is a good starting point). I select pages at random from the news, sports, and "living" sections, or from any section that seems to include interesting features. Students skim these pages, front and back, and identify one or two articles that interest them.

I then give a brief explanation of syllabic prosodies, relying on Lewis Turco's *Poetry: An Introduction through Writing* (Reston Publishing, 1973) to provide examples of poems written in normative syllabics (a poem in which all lines have the same number of syllables) or in quantitative syllabics (poems in which the poet varies the syllable count in each line of the first stanza but makes the lines of succeeding stanzas correspond to the syllable count established in the first stanza). With appropriate examples, students can readily count syllables and understand the distinction between the two forms. They also begin to see how the pace of reading is partially determined by the number of syllables the poet chooses for the lines.

To experience the task the poet faces, I ask students to make a poem out of a section of the newspaper article they found interesting, using either normative or quantitative syllabics. Students are free to add or delete words to help the pattern or the meaning. I urge them to experiment with line length and to judge for themselves what happens when different words are chosen to end or begin a line.

Since students do not feel the pressure of having to generate material from within themselves, they willingly experiment with combinations of words that someone else has written. They begin to see, firsthand, that placement of words and length of line make a poem dull as well as exciting.

Here are two poems which a student wrote, using an article from a sports page as a starting point.

(Quantitative syllabics)

The premier duck and tens of thousands of
Canadian geese
And snow-white
swans
Raft up by the thousands

Hunters don full suits and get into the
Icy water chill
Arms and legs
Ache
Face and fingers grow numb

Amidst their decoys waves splash icy cold
Water into the
Booter's suit
Ducks
Brush over their scalps and die.

(Normative syllabics)

The premier ducks and
tens of thousands of
Canadian geese
And snow-white swans, raft
up by the thousands

Hunters don full suits
and get into the
icy cold water
Chilly arms and legs
Ache. Face and fingers
grow numb and turn blue

Amidst their decoys,
Waves splash icy cold
water into the

> Booter's suit while ducks
> Brush over their scalps
> And die with a shot.

> Ann Shepherd

The teacher may not judge the poems created in this fashion to be masterpieces, but the students have experienced a poetic form rather than simply observed it. They begin to understand, too, the differences between a newspaper article and a poem, differences which teachers sometimes talk about but rarely help students to perceive for themselves.

Clozing the Gap

In teaching the reading or writing of poetry, English teachers rightly emphasize the poet's ability to choose the *mot juste*, the right word for the context. Too often, though, we simply ask, "Why do you think the poet used that word there?" That question is important but it does not involve students directly. Consider, instead, a method that relies on a rudimentary form of the cloze procedure.

Many reading specialists use the cloze procedure to diagnose reading difficulties. Briefly, in this procedure a word or a phrase is omitted from a sentence and the student is asked to supply the appropriate word or phrase demanded by the context. The procedure can become complex in the hands of a reading specialist, but the classroom teacher with no preparation in the teaching of reading can use it in a poetry class for nondiagnostic purposes.

During one class session I distributed a copy of "Daybreak," a poem from Gary Soto's *The Elements of San Joaquin* (University of Pittsburgh Press, 1977) from which I had omitted several words:

> Daybreak

> In this moment when the light starts up
> In the east and _____
> The horizon until it catches fire,

> We enter the fields to hoe,
> Row after row, among the small _____ of onion,
> Waving off the dragonflies
> That _____ the air.

> And tears the onions raise
> Do not begin in your eyes but in ours,
> In the salt _____
> From one blister into another;

They begin in knowing
You will never waken to hear
The hour timed to a _____ _____ ,
The wind pressing us closer to the ground.

When the season ends,
And the onions are _____ from their sleep,
We won't forget what you failed to see,
And nothing will heal
Under the rain's _____ fingers.

Gary Soto

I then asked students to list the words they thought might fit the blanks. Next, I asked them to form small groups and discuss the appropriateness of their choices. Finally, I asked them to re-assemble in a large group. I announced that the words Soto had chosen, in order, were "rubs," "flags," "ladder," "blown," "heart beat," "unplugged," and "broken." Since students had tried to identify appropriate words themselves, they were now very interested in determining how the poet's words worked—how, for example, the noun "ladder" became a verb to create the pattern of dragonflies.

By repeating the procedure with other poems, students become increasingly perceptive about the dimensions of words that poets pay attention to—sound values, the actions that verbs suggest, the appeal of some words to visual and tactile senses, the ways words work together (e.g., alliteration)—in short, most of the "tricks" a poet uses. This use of the cloze procedure helps students feel that they have discovered something about poetry for themselves, not just listened to the teacher's judgment on why the poet chose a particular word.

A variation is to ask students to compose their own poems and to bring them to small discussion groups with words omitted. The group must decide what word the student used in the original poem. Students enjoy the "guessing game," but the method has other advantages. The fledgling poet experiences firsthand the reaction of his or her readers and thus gains a genuine sense of "audience." And as students propose words to fill in the blanks, the poet may learn that some of these suggestions work better than the ones he or she chose originally. In this way, students experience directly the value of revision.

Finally, the cloze procedure can be used to teach most poetic devices inductively. By choosing appropriate poems and omitting appropriate words, the teacher can help a class discover the values of assonance, end rhyme, onomatopoeia, and other devices.

In all of these activities, the teacher becomes less of a lecturer to passive recipients than a creator of opportunities through which students make personal discoveries about the richness of a most precious natural resource, their own language. They become involved at one and the same time with discipline and with play. They become, in a word, poets.

4 Getting Involved in Research

"Yes, But...":
The Student and the Literary Research Paper

Sue Howell
Carbondale (Illinois) Community High School

Several years ago, I sat in on an informal discussion led by Ken Macrorie, who had just spoken at the annual Illinois Association of Teachers of English convention on the topic of teaching writing. Those who had remained after the formal speech were, like myself, Macrorie fans. We all wanted to talk (all at once) about our students and our experiences with student-centered writing. One refrain, however, kept recurring: "Yes, but . . ." Is it possible, this refrain asked, to maintain a student-centered approach to writing within a curriculum with fairly rigid requirements—some of which we might have qualms about abandoning? For example, the research paper. We know how important it is for students to "speak in honest voices and tell the truth." Yet how can we reconcile this imperative with the demands of an assignment like the conventional research paper? How about something different? Macrorie suggested. Not exactly research, but "I-search"—a paper that records the student's exploration of an absorbing topic. A paper that describes a process rather than the results of that process. I left the convention determined to try such an assignment with one of my junior English classes.

I had some definite ideas about what I wanted from this type of assignment. First, I wanted students to do a great deal of reading. And I wanted them to read in the general area of imaginative literature rather than about their current preoccupations—rock stars, astrology, and demonic possession. As to whether an assignment on a restricted topic can be "student-centered," I believe that it can. I think that one of our primary functions as teachers is to help students into awareness of themselves, of others, of the world around them. This is what literature is all about. We can help students see possibilities for exploration and discovery that they do not immediately see themselves. Turning students loose in the library is not giving them freedom. On the other hand, if we give them some idea of what's out there, afford the opportunities to taste and sample, and suggest writers and topics that might be particularly interesting to them, we enable them to make meaningful choices, rather than limiting them to the accidents of their environment.

As I envisioned this assignment, students would explore a particular literary topic. They would engage in the activities of analysis and synthesis normally associated with the "research" paper. They would ask themselves questions and look for the answers. They would express their tentative conclusions on paper and use those conclusions as the basis for further exploration. I saw several important differences between this assignment and the standard literary research paper. First, students would not be required to assume the role of expert, the mask of "objectivity." They would be encouraged to write as themselves, reacting thoughtfully and honestly to the literature. As explorers, they wouldn't worry too much about whether they were contradicting themselves ("A foolish consistency . . ."). Second, the process of exploration would be the subject of the final paper. This paper might record false starts, blind alleys, misconceptions—the sort of thing we usually leave out when we turn in our neatly typed pages. A deeper awareness of the nature of the research process should enable students to become more active participants in that process. They might come to at least a partial understanding of what "research" really is. With all this in mind, I designed the assignment.

As a preliminary to the "I-search" assignment, students prepared oral reports and bibliographies on writers of their own choosing. The purpose of this activity was to inform the class of some of the possible topics open to them. The bibliographies were made available to any student wishing to follow up on a particular topic. I told the class that they were going to do a "different" type of research paper, one which emphasized the discoveries they made through reading. I suggested four types of topics:

1. The life and work of a particular writer
2. A particular theme (novels of war, women in literature)
3. A type, genre, or period (political satire, folklore)
4. Questions (What happens when a book is made into a movie? What kinds of books did people read in the 1920s?)

During the early stages of their investigations, students wrote two short papers. The first was an explanation of their choice of topic and a tentative statement of purpose (which included questions to be answered in the course of the investigation). The second was a review of what they already knew about this topic. These papers would later be incorporated into the final paper.

The *sine qua non* of this assignment was that the final paper be an honest record of the students' experiences. I gave the class detailed instructions to help them lay the groundwork. They all owned copies of *Writing Research Papers* (Scott, Foresman, 1976); I left it to them to ferret out whatever information they needed about mechanics, footnotes, and so on. What I continued to emphasize was the process of their investigations and the recording of that process:

(Photocopied handout)

1. You should be taking notes (pp. 36–51 WRP). Sometimes you may jot down notes as you read, perhaps recording interesting quotations. (Don't forget to get the page number.) Whenever you finish reading a selection, jot down personal impressions, main points, summaries. Your notes will be of two types:
   a. Notes relating to the purposes of your paper that you set out in your planning paper. You will want to jot down responses relating to the questions you raised about your topic.
   b. Notes describing anything in your reading which especially interested you.
   Date your notes! They must be turned in with your paper.
2. Structure. Most papers of this type require a formal structure. This paper, however, will have an INFORMAL structure. Here are two types of informal organization:
   a. Diary. This is a week-by-week record of your search: what your goals were, what you thought you'd find out, how you went about your search, what discoveries—and mistakes —you made.
   b. Narrative. This is a bit more structured than a diary. You are not necessarily describing what you did in chronological order. You might set the paper up this way:
   (1) Why I chose the topic
   (2) What I already knew
   (3) What I wanted to find out
   (4) How I got information
   (5) What I read, and what I thought about it
   (6) What I discovered
3. You will need a formal bibliography at the end of your paper (pp. 119-135 WRP).
4. As for footnotes, use them as needed (pp. 13-118 WRP). Place all footnotes on a separate page at the end of the paper.
   Read pp. 59-74 WRP on incorporating quotations.

> Remember: This paper is a record of your experiences and thoughts. You must use enough detail to communicate this.

Although these "I-search" papers did not represent the last critical word on American literature, they did represent honest attempts on the part of students to deal with literature on their own terms. One of the most positive results of the assignment was that it allowed students to speak for themselves in their own voices—a necessary first step, I believe, towards real involvement with the material. When students discussed their reasons for choosing a particular topic, they made the initial connection between themselves as readers and the literature they would read:

> . . . the main reason that I chose Paine for this paper is because . . . my own personal values and beliefs in religion and other things are almost identical to those of Thomas Paine.

> To a professional soldier [this student's chosen career] it is immensely important to have a great and varied knowledge of strategies and tactics; thus my reading of war novels.

The fact that students were not forced to assume the role of "expert," and "objective" mask, meant that they could use the paper as an exploratory tool, making tentative statements, discarding hasty conclusions, following their thoughts on paper:

> I began my I-search by reading an assortment of Stephen Crane's short stories. I felt this was the best way of gaining an understanding of what type of person he was. Throughout my investigation, I kept this thought in mind: When you read a story, you are also reading a person, the life and feelings of the author. Later . . . I would read what the critics thought of his works, but I wanted to get my own impression first.

> I read *Five Smooth Stones* by Anne Fairbairn, hoping it would give me a start on my paper. However, . . . I discovered her point of view seemed to be that of a man! Therefore, since I was looking for the development of women's ideas in literature, Anne Fairbairn didn't seem appropriate.

Such reflections, of course, take place whenever one writes an investigative paper. Ordinarily, they are the prelude to the paper and not the paper itself. By making these explorations part of their papers, however, students brought the total process of investigation, analysis, and synthesis into focus for themselves, gaining a greater awareness of what it was that they were doing:

> When I first read her poetry, I could not understand any of it. But after I finished reading *The Poet and Her Book* and understood the traumas, tragedies, and experiences of her life, her poetry made . . . sense.

> I was very excited this week to find similarities between the views of the critics and myself concerning Crane's stories. I often wanted to go back and read the stories again. . . .

The papers reflected a relatively high degree of involvement on the part of students. I believe that this is because the assignment was, in effect, theirs rather than mine:

> . . . many times the reading would carry my thoughts to a far-off battlefield or to some steamy jungle clutching the body of a wounded comrade. . . .

> Martha asked me if I would like to go hear Gwendolyn Brooks read her poetry in Mt. Vernon. Sure, it would be something interesting to do. . . . Her voice defined her words. Picture after picture came into my head as she read. I could see the ugly little Lincoln ("The Life of Lincoln West"), the dirty halls of the Mecca building, the white picket fence the little girl had to stay behind after 9:00. . . . I reread her poetry and began to really have a grasp of what she was communicating.

And most students eventually moved on to more "objective" analysis:

> Knowles seems to feel there is a fine line dividing goodness and insanity. All of the characters he portrays as being good are also thought to be crazy. Maybe Knowles is trying to say that today's world cannot believe in true goodness from any person because we are so used to the bad.

These analyses, however, were not merely exercises in finding "hidden meanings"; instead, each was the end product of a student's experience with the work. And because students had become more aware of the dynamics of literary experience, students felt more comfortable with their own opinions and conclusions.

The conclusions students drew were not necessarily those that would be drawn by mature readers. But they were the conclusions of readers growing in awareness:

> Why, if we as Americans possess the most perfect society in all the world, do we complain so much?

> I've been exposed to where the blacks are coming from. They
> don't need whites to tell them their work is good . . . their own
> sisters and brothers want to tell them, and they want to hear
> from them. . . .

Too often the literary research paper, at least on the high school level, is a sterile exercise that encourages teaching about literature rather than literature itself. Students are asked to abstract and generalize beyond their capacities, and thus they develop an unhealthy reliance on the opinions of others in their search for something to say. An assignment of the type I have described, however, emphasizes the importance of the student's experience in relation to what he or she reads. Students learn to respect their own responses and to express themselves honestly. They also learn, of course, the usual techniques we associate with research—summary, synthesis, the mechanics of footnotes, and so on. Most important, however, they learn something about learning—that mysterious process which depends so much on the activity of the self, on the searching "I."

The Interview as a Practical Research Model

William F. Woods
Wichita State University

Few students enter a writing class ready to write a research paper. Even if they know how to take notes and organize them, they seldom understand what it means to work on a research *problem*. Our job as teachers, then, is to show students how to explore new subjects by building on knowledge they already possess. If we can help them identify and develop their present conceptual and investigative skills, they can proceed on their own to refine these techniques as they engage new subjects and begin to write about them.

One way to acquaint students with basic research skills is to assign an interview paper. Writing the interview allows them to use their already developed social skills to elicit responses from interviewees and to evaluate or draw conclusions from what they have heard. In essence, an interview is a dialogue between the researcher and another person. As such, it is not unlike the "dialectic" that scholars carry on with their data; in both cases, the researcher engages in that process of question and answer, of probing and evaluating, that constitutes any kind of inquiry. In short, by writing the interview, students develop the same skills necessary to writing the research paper. Later on, the experience students have had with the interview can be used as a paradigm for teaching the process of inquiry that forms the basis of the research paper.

Preparing students for writing the interview paper means helping them do the necessary groundwork before that first meeting with the subject. Generally, the interviewer is expected to choose the subject, and so the first question is *who?* Then there are the mechanics of setting up the meeting, taking notes, and deciding what in the world to talk about. My own instructions to the students go something like the following.

Choosing a Subject

Begin with people you know. Friends of the family or people at work make the assignment easier because you already know a great deal about them, and you are familiar with their surroundings —their "context." Better yet, these people know you and will probably volunteer information about themselves that you didn't even think of asking. If the subject is not an acquaintance, find out something about that person in advance. If the interview will focus on the person's job, find out about the company and its employees. You can collect this background information by asking around or by spending a couple of hours in the library. For example, if you are interviewing a nurse, look through several issues of *Nursing* or *Nursing Forum*. The important thing is to get a general sense of what your subject's job is like before you ask him or her about it. In a formal research paper, this preliminary background search is called establishing the context for the study.

Setting Up the Interview

For some interviews, an appointment is absolutely necessary. (For instance, when one of my students interviewed the City Manager of Wichita, Kansas, she had to make an appointment two weeks ahead of time. But calling ahead paid off; the Manager gave her a full half hour, and she was able to ask some involved questions about the city's government.) Setting up the meeting ahead of time also makes it easier to find the person in his or her characteristic surroundings. As a general rule, a person's home or place of work tells us a good deal about his or her life, and after all, that's the main purpose of the interview. One last note on appointments: if the first meeting is held at the person's convenience, it may be possible to ask for a second interview. Depending on the length of the paper and the complexity of the material, this second discussion might be crucial.

Taking Notes

Most people won't mind if an interviewer records the discussion on a pad, but other methods are sometimes necessary. If the interviewer finds it hard to keep up with the flow, writing down key words and phrases might be the best solution. Of course there is always the question of whether to use a tape recorder. Portable units can usually be checked out from the audiovisual office, and there's nothing like a tape for getting down exactly what the person said. However, some people are made nervous by a whirring tape recorder, and often it is difficult to locate the parts you want in a tape that might run as long as an hour. Ultimately, the interviewer has to decide what method works best in his or her own case. The main think is to record as much as you can, and to sit down immediately after the interview and write out at length the important parts before you forget them.

Prepared Questions

There are good reasons for bringing prepared questions to the interview. First, the interviewee may not feel like talking that day, and unless you are well informed about the focus you have selected for the interview, you may find it hard to invent appropriate questions on the spot. Second, and perhaps even more important, your time with that person is limited; if you aren't able to steer the discussion away from small talk, you may find yourself walking away from the interview with only a few general remarks.

It is useful to divide your questions into three groups:

1. *Identify the person's basis of authority.* Your first questions should lay the groundwork for the rest of the discussion by establishing the person's identity and relationship to his or her surroundings. For example, if the person sells chickens to fast-food restaurants, as did the subject of one student's interview, you want to find out how long he has sold poultry, where and when he sells it, and how successfully. It makes a difference, in other words, whether you're getting the opinions of a big-city poultry dealer or someone who sells a few chickens on Saturdays.

2. *Get the facts—in depth.* The need for getting detailed "background" information about the person can't be overemphasized. Throughout the interview, you will have the chance to ask questions about the details of the person's life and work, but you will ask better, more specific questions if you already have them in hand, neatly typed out, if possible. When it comes time to write up the interview, you will be able to provide that detailed glimpse of "real life" which readers enjoy in any piece of writing.

3. *Get a clear picture of the person's ideas.* You can't really know what the person will say before it comes out in the discussion, but you can and should prepare yourself to follow up on ideas and opinions when they emerge. And if the person doesn't volunteer a point of view, it's your job to ask. In fact, you must be ready to suggest ways for the person to talk about his or her ideas. For example, you can ask the person to analyze a problem, to explain the causes of a situation, to trace the history of some of his or her interests. Often, the person will use a particular phrase or expression which seems to sum up a point of view; try to record the exact wording of such key phrases, and make some notes to yourself on how that phrase was meant.

The steps I have outlined for preparing for an interview correspond roughly to the beginning stages of a research project: the investigator senses a problematic situation or conflict, states the problem by specifying what *kinds* of things have to be known in order to explain the conflict, and finally devises a set of questions with which to explore the problem. These leading (or "heuristic") questions provide new information and new perspectives on the problem and thereby prepare the investigator to formulate a hypothesis or possible solution. The same function is performed by the interviewer's questions, both the prepared ones and those that arise spontaneously. Using these questions, the interviewer tries to open up perspectives into the interviewee's character, situation, and attitudes—material which later makes it possible to create a vivid, rounded, meaningful account of that person's life experience.

The next step in the process of inquiry, as in interviewing, is to arrive at the hypothesis, or meaningful statement about the subject. Unfortunately there is no rule we can follow, either to formulate a hypothesis about a problem or to derive a meaningful statement about the subject of an interview. Still, there are general guidelines. In problem solving, an investigator tries to match known concepts with the problem situation, hoping to explain the new pattern as a transformation or variation of an old one. In writing an interview, we can employ another kind of pattern in an attempt to give shape to the information supplied. This pattern has five parts.

Arriving on the Scene

Writing an interview is like writing a narrative, insofar as one is describing an interaction between two people, providing a setting for that action, and devising ways of introducing the readers into this "scene" at the beginning and leading them out of it at the end. Here we are concerned with the beginning. The main function of the beginning is to help the reader become accustomed to looking over the writer's shoulder, so to speak. Perhaps the easiest way for the writer to do this is to describe his or her own entry onto the scene—the arrival at the person's home or the drive out to the job.

Conveying a Sense of the Character

The heart of any interview is our sense of the subject's character, which emerges from overt comments by the writer, from the person's movements, gestures, anecdotes and opinions, and even from oblique hints, such as this brief description of two dogs:

> At 1:15 I turned into the driveway and was promptly greeted by two German Shepherds barking furiously. However, by the time I had stopped the car, they were both standing on their hind legs looking in the driver's window and wagging their tails. This was my welcome to the home of Beth-Anne Chard, who greeted me at the door and warmly accepted me into her home. (Shirley Leftwich)

Perhaps the most common technique for conveying character, however, is the direct description of what the person *does* during the interview. This ongoing description keeps us from losing our sense of the person's presence in the scene; it might also be called a "narrative line" because it holds the interview together, providing a frame for the anecdotes and background information which make up the discussion. The following example from an interview with a child in a reform school shows how the writer can convey the person's character while at the same time introducing matters for discussion:

> We sat down on the floor in the hall, and she pulled a cigarette out of her tiny purse and lit it. Deciding that the best choice would be to ignore it, I began by asking her why she had to go to court in the first place.

"Shoplifting" was her answer and given with a really "cute" smile. I am sure that the look on my face belied my answer of "Oh yeah." I was mortified. She looked very young, so I asked her how old she was. She told me that she was eleven years old and that she had done about everything, including stabbing her cat with a fork. (Dana Decker)

The Cargo of Information

Aside from the fascination of glimpsing another person's life, the interview's main source of power is its promise of information—the facts, the inside story, the distilled wisdom of a person's life and work. As Aristotle tells us, however, the trick is to mingle instruction with delight—in this case, to make sure the new material retains the flavor of the experiences and the outlook peculiar to that person. Probably the most effective way to introduce this substantive material is simply to record the person's anecdotes. People find it natural to explain matters by telling stories about themselves and others (the rhetorical term is *exempla*, or "parables"), and as long as the narrative line or sense of scene is maintained, the writer can build a strong interview from such tales.

Anecdotes are not the only method of conveying information about the character's job or primary interests. For short periods, the writer can step in and relate the pertinent facts directly to the reader. The only requirements are that the information should add to our understanding of the person interviewed, and that these facts generate their own interest.

The interview's utility as a vehicle for information is its most obvious similarity to the research paper, and, to be sure, the material for many research projects is gathered primarily through interviews. Less obvious, perhaps, is the resemblance between the researcher's exploration, or analysis of his subject, and the way the writer of an interview explores the character and life-experience of a person by focusing on significant details such as a reform school child's smoking habits. In such cases, the writer is actually using methods of rhetorical invention, trying to "discover" the best ways to explain a subject.

The Time Dimension

Supplying information about a job or other experience opens up one sort of perspective on a person's life. But a further dimension can be added by drawing out the relationship between that person's past experience and his or her present conditions. Call it the time dimension, a sense of history, or just "roots"—the effect is the same: the reader begins to see a meaningful pattern in the person's life as it develops over a period of years. It is just this sense of purpose in a life, and perhaps even more, the fulfillment and clarification of a purpose, that arises from the best interviews and allows them to make a statement worthy of the person they describe. Here is such a statement about Jim Banks, a mechanic:

> "I don't know how I got started," he added. "I have been a mechanic around the country most of my life, the past 25 or 30 years, and I just decided that I wanted an old car. So in 1955, I bought a Model T Ford and restored it, and I've been buying and restoring ever since."
> As Jim has pointed out, restoring can sometimes be expensive and is always time-consuming, but the final result is worth the effort. It is gratifying to take a rusty, broken-down piece of junk, and through diligent, hard work, turn it into a masterpiece. "It's like saving a piece of history," Jim Banks said quietly, "and if we don't do it, they'll be gone forever. They won't be coming back."
> (Jerry Glessner)

The "statement" the interviewer makes about the person's life is best described as supplying a perspective in time, but really it is more like the fundamental "theme" of the interview, drawing strength from all the other parts. For unless the writer's treatment of the person's character and occupation have prepared us for a long retrospective look, we won't get the desired sense of inevitability as we see the person arriving finally at his or her present condition after years of effort. This sense of a basic pattern emerging in a person's life is probably the most difficult effect for an interviewer to achieve. Nevertheless, by trying to achieve it, writers cease to be mere takers of notes and become *interpreters* of experience, on a par with research workers, whose hypotheses, or new statements about the facts, are simply another kind of interpretation.

Leaving the Interview

Ending an interview presents the same problems as ending a piece of fiction: one has to avoid the "bump" when the reader falls out of the story on the last page. It is possible simply to end with the person's answer to the last question, but if the writer has maintained a sense of "scene," has conveyed the dynamics of an interaction between two people, it is best to give their discussion a sense of closure. One way to do this is to show the interviewer leaving the person's home, glancing back on it, or thinking about it in order to give the reader a way of holding the interview in memory. Here is how Linda Jones ended her interview with Fout the Gravedigger:

> Then, quite unexpectedly, my interviewed subject took off his frayed brim grey hat and shaking my hand tightly, said, "Thank *you*, Mizz Jones. You've made my day." I glanced in the rear-view mirror as I waited for a break in the traffic to enter the street. Fout was still leaning against the service gate, his hat still dangling from his hand.

In summary, a chief advantage of the interview as an introductory research model is that it brings the student directly into contact with the material. Then it puts to use life-long training in carrying out question-and-answer routines, sifting the evidence, and drawing conclusions about the motives, experience, and personality of another person. The teacher's task is to guide the student in applying and extending these skills by providing general guidelines like those suggested above and by pointing out analogies between the process of interviewing and the process of inquiry which will form the basis for the research paper.

References

Grobel, Larry. "A Star Interview Is Born." *Writer's Digest* 57 (January 1978): 19–23.

Townsend, R. C. "The Possibilities of Field Work." *College English* 34 (1973): 481–99.

Zinsser, William. "The Interview." In *On Writing Well: An Informal Guide to Writing Nonfiction*. New York: Harper and Row, 1976, pp. 68–80.

Untangling the Skein of Names

John L. Idol, Jr.
Clemson University

Few students can confidently and accurately explain the meaning of their given names, much less their surnames, despite the fact that digging for one's roots has recently become the American pastime. Even in the family-conscious South, where I have taught at both the secondary and the college levels, only a handful of students have ever explored the meaning of the words that they have answered to since the day they became aware of what their parents called them. Fewer still can explain why their home town or home county bears its name. Rarer still are those students who can give solid information about the names printed on the products they buy. Prodded to think for a few mintues about the long string of names they have encountered since they toddled off to nursery school, students soon conclude that most of us are tangled in an ever-growing skein of names. By sending my college freshmen to libraries, by asking them to talk to or write to town and county officials, and by encouraging them to sit down to query their kinfolk and neighbors, I try to help my students unravel their personal, and our common, skein of names.

My project has three phases and attempts to answer three questions: Who am I? Where do I live? What do I buy? Each phase is designed to include as many informants as possible.

As soon as I call the class roll in the second semester of freshman English, I pose the first question. I ask my students to tell me and the class what their surnames mean. Usually, only three or four in a class of twenty-five have exact knowledge. Knowing that will be the case, I select five or six names to comment upon as I call the roll. Almost without exception, students show a lively interest in what their classmates and I say.

Capitalizing upon their desire to learn more about their names, I make the first assignment: Discover the meaning of both your given name and surname by talking to your kinfolk, by researching your name in the library, or by writing an expert on names. As soon as you can, come back to class and tell us not only what your surname is but what kind of surname it is (locational, occupational, patronymic, or other, such as nickname), how far back you can trace the name (not the family tree), and to what ethnic group it belongs. Also share with everyone the meaning of your given name(s).

To launch their investigation, I urge students to telephone or write the dedicated old aunt or retired grandfather who is now doing the family history. I list such books as Flora Loughead's *Dictionary of Given Names*, Basil Cottle's *The Penguin Dictionary of Surnames*, P. H. Reaney's *A Dictionary of British Surnames*, Elsdon Smith's *New Dictionary of American Family Names*, Max Gottschald's *Deutsche Namenkunde*, Albert Dauzat's *Dictionnaire des noms de famille et prénoms de France*, and Fra Angelico Chavez's *Origins of New Mexico Families* and suggest that similar books for other national groups can be found in the same area in the library. Finally, I offer them the address of some authority should they need to write an expert.

Experience has taught me that one of the most eagerly awaited days in the semester is the day when students give oral, documented reports on the discoveries made about their names. What will be revealed by such people as Coburn, Lautenschlager, Hogg. Larousse, or Polonski? And students repeatedly report that the information is as eagerly received at home as in the classroom, except in those few homes where Aunt Gertrude or Grandfather Himmelfarb has already spread the news about the family name.

While students are discovering something about who they are, I initiate the second phase, learning about the area where they live. This project becomes the topic for their term paper and, accordingly, is closely coordinated with their study of research techniques as covered in their textbook. Here, briefly, is how I get the project started.

I ask students to order a highway map for their home county or parish from the appropriate state government department (usually the Department of Transportation) and instruct them to list every village, town, or city shown on the map. Next they classify these names by deciding whether they are descriptive, personal, possessive, commemorative, or incident names. (If their classification is wrong, subsequent research will lead them to make corrections.)

They then choose twenty or twenty-five names for further research, the goal being to discover when the selected village, town,
or city received its name, who named it, for whom it was named if
the place does not bear a descriptive name, and whether the place
has ever borne another name. To provide a geographical frame for
the places they will discuss, I require my students to write a brief
history of the county or parish where the places they are investigating are located. A two-page history is usually adequate.

Once more they are encouraged to depend upon as much personal communication as possible. Given the chance to discover their
best sources, students will ultimately find that most counties or
parishes have historical commissions, journalists interested in local
names, postmasters with considerable information about the
places where they work, elders in the family or community with
many facts and much lore, local historians who will gladly spend
an afternoon sharing their interests, and county officials who
have learned much about the areas they serve or represent. In time
they will also come upon such organizations as the American
Name Society and learn through it that almost every state has a
resident expert on place names; they will discover such books as
Kelsie Harder's *Illustrated Dictionary of Place Names*, Myron
Quimby's *Scratch Ankle, U.S.A.*, and George Stewart's *American
Place-Names*; and they will find, in many cases, that there are
books or periodicals devoted to names in the various states.

Another discovery, for students an unexpected one, is that
many people enjoy talking about place names and that, further,
officials of local historical associations and librarians in local
towns or high schools often want copies of their completed term
papers. Knowing that their studies will be shared by fellow citizens
back home gives many students a new sense of responsibility
about writing.

One of the intriguing challenges of this project is having to
separate fact from lore, since not every place name can be pinned
down with absolute certainty and since local informants have,
at times, conflicting explanations of how a name was chosen.

As in the project involving personal names, class response is
again keen when oral reports are made about place names. Individual research has proven to them by the time of the reports that
interesting, often fascinating, stories lie behind place names, and
most students are as eager to receive information as they are to
give it. In the interest of time, not every place name is covered in

the oral report. A good number for each student is four or five. Students from the same county or parish can be asked to present different names.

The stages of preparation for a term paper on place names do not essentially differ from those on other topics, be they self-chosen or assigned. What is different is that students draw upon personal interviews and letters in addition to books and periodicals. This difference in sources requires the mastery of more types of bibliographical forms and thus, from a teacher's point of view, constitutes a valuable learning experience. But, generally speaking, a term paper on place names can easily be meshed with the traditional research techniques outlined in rhetoric books.

The third project, discovering the denotative and connotative meanings of trade names, offers a potentially larger subject of study and must, therefore, be carefully planned before it is assigned. One workable scheme is to assign each student a particular kind of product: automobiles, candy bars, cereals, perfumes, athletic shoes, soaps, shaving creams, cigarettes, toilet tissue, phonograph records. If the subject assigned is not agreeable, students can switch among themselves or devise new topics until everyone is happy.

The next steps are simple ones. First of all, students visit local shops, department stores, car dealers, or merchants and, notepad in hand, record the names of products they find. If they choose slack times to make their visits, they can often elicit information from clerks and merchants and engage in some speculation about why, among athletic shoes for example, one brand is named the Jayhawk, another the Montreal, another the Puma, another the Elite, another the Vantage. Later, with the aid of a good dictionary, students will attempt to analyze what each name denotes. Next comes a period of speculation about the connotative range of meanings.

The final step is writing an analytic paper, which will be read in part or in full to the class. The paper resulting from the research for the meanings of trade names arouses the interest of every student, and with good reason. Students have been bombarded by trade names since they were old enough to understand what products beckoned to them between the adventures of Donald Duck and Captain Kangaroo. They have been consumers for years before entering the college classroom, and they have sometimes thought why one product appealed to them and another left them cold, even though both products had similar costs and records of performance or acceptance. Briefly, they recognize that words have acted upon them and that they now have a chance to examine why they may have reacted as they did. This third project thus reveals the competitive world of swirling words. To afford students an opportunity to see how massive that swirl is, I ask them to look into Ellen Crowley's *Trade Names Dictionary*.

A follow-up exercise to the paper on trade names is to write an advertisement for a hypothetical new product. To a generation brought up on a hot medium, huckstering seems natural, yet some of their most insightful criticism of the writing efforts of their classmates emerges here. And they get about as much help as they give, for they are displaying their writing wares before a knowing—if somewhat jaded—audience.

One comforting thought about these three projects is that each can continue to serve students outside the classroom. To their daughters and sons, they can one day pass along information about the names they give them; to their friends, neighbors, and families, as well as to strangers, they can explain why towns in their native counties have certain names; and to themselves and to their kinfolk and friends they can reveal something about the sway words have when chosen to do a particular job in the marketplace.

A second long-lasting benefit, one that can often be shared, is the list of books and periodicals and the names of informants put together by students during their study of names. Future encounters with names of towns, streets, rivers, mountains, hotels, teams, products, and people should leave them with the comfortable feeling that they are not helplessly entangled in names nor blithely ignorant of their importance.

The Research Paper as Problem-Solving

Carol Carpenter
Detroit Institute of Technology

Since my students are not English majors, the traditional topics and approaches to writing the research paper failed. Yet, I felt it was important that they learn to investigate a research question fully and to write an analytic paper. Since our faculty stresses the interrelationship of disciplines, it seemed to me that the research paper offered an opportunity for our students to practice an interdisciplinary approach.

Instead of limiting students to literary research, they were encouraged to investigate any field. The requirement was, in fact, that they do library as well as original research (i.e., interviews, surveys, experiments, case studies). They were also asked to incorporate personal experience and to use at least one piece of literature. To integrate library research, original research, personal experience, and a literary source was, indeed, a demanding task for college freshmen.

To help students deal with the usual difficulties in research, I wrote up the problems that students were encountering and presented them to the class in eight problem-solving exercises. They tackled problems progressively, beginning with the selection of a topic and ending with evaluation. They are presented here just as they were presented to the class.

Exercise 1: Research Project—Selecting a Question

One of the most difficult parts of a research project is finding a topic that's interesting and challenging. You'll read, write, think, talk, dream about this question. It'll become your best friend/ worst enemy. So, it's important to select a question you can live with. To help you in this selection process, work through the exercises described below.

1. List ten topics that you think students in the class might be interested in researching. You may select topics from any field. Now, pose a specific question about each of these topics.
2. Complete the following open-ended statements.
   a. If I had a chance, I'd like to find out why . . .
   b. If I could study something just for fun, I'd study . . .
   c. In my spare time, I . . .
   d. People might behave differently if they knew more about . . .
   e. As I grow older, I question . . .
3. Form a group with several classmates and brainstorm questions that might be asked about education. Write down these questions and examine them in terms of suitable research topics. Next, each group member will pose a topic in a different field. Brainstorm questions that might be asked about that topic. Are any of these suitable for research questions?

Exercise 2: Research Project—Starting the Search

Directions: Selecting a research question was a mind-wracking process. Now you've decided on the question and started your research, but you may find that unexpected problems hinder your progress:

1. Knowing where and how to start researching your question.
2. Finding too many/too few written materials.
3. Thinking you can't/shouldn't meet a part of the assignment.
4. Wondering how you can integrate original research, library research, personal experience, and literature.

Don't let these problems discourage you. They mean you're actually beginning your research. It never hurts, however, to ask classmates and the instructor to become involved in such problems. By looking at someone else's difficulties and sharing your own, you may find the answer to questions that are nagging you. In addition, practice in problem-solving helps you learn to generate and analyze alternatives. And the realization that there are alternatives reduces that helpless feeling, that conviction that you'll never complete the research project to the instructor's satisfaction.

146   *Getting Involved in Research*

Instead, you'll come to see that the research project is *your* project, your opportunity to do creative investigation and to aid others with their investigation.

Based on a premise of "creative investigation," I've posed five problems based on projects with which students in this class are currently involved. It's your job to "solve" these problems. To do this:

1. Form a group.
2. Assume that you are the student in one of the situations described.
3. State the student's problem clearly.
4. Brainstorm possible solutions. Do not eliminate any solutions, even those that appear to be absurd.
5. Analyze each solution. Consider its feasibility and consequences.
6. What solution(s) does your group suggest and why?
7. Be prepared to present and explain your suggested solution(s) to the class.

Use this method throughout exercises 2–8.

You've got the following problem:

1. Your question is "What relationship exists between violence in sports and violence in spectators?" You want very much to do your research in this field, but you can't seem to find any books, magazines, or journals that deal directly with your topic.
2. You're interested in the attitudes of police officers, especially their attitudes about dealing with marijuana users. You want to compare/contrast suburban and city police officers. Yet such a study seems overwhelming, and you don't know where and how to begin your research.
3. You've been interested in your family's history ever since you were a child and your grandmother told you stories about the family. You've got easy access to cooperative family members; however, the assignment also requires library research. You don't think library research is relevant or will add anything to your project.
4. You are an engineering student and a race car builder and driver. This research project offers you the opportunity to

investigate and design a new suspension system that you've been thinking about for a long time. You have no difficulty finding engineering journals and engineers to interview. But a required part of the assignment is to use a piece of literature, and you don't know how you can possibly meet this requirement.

5. You've decided to investigate the causes and effects of teenage drinking. You find, however, that so much material has been written about the subject that you don't know where to begin. You're afraid that you'll miss reading an important study; you know you can't read all the books and magazines, and you don't know where to start. No matter where you start, you don't know how to select the "important" information.

Exercise 3: Research Project—Taking Notes

You've got the following problem:

1. You've checked out an armload of books, and you skim through them for background information about your topic. It is time-consuming to take notes, and yet you might want to use some of this material later in your paper.

2. You think taking notes on note cards is a needless bother and you'd like to find a more effective/efficient method.

3. You have two problems. (a) You've found a quote you'd like to use, but your author is quoting someone else. Do you need to go to the original source? If not, how do you indicate in your notes that you're quoting a quote? (b) You're using only one article from a book of articles. Which comes first on your bibliography card—the editor of the book or the author of the article?

4. You're getting information from an interview you've conducted. Should excerpts from or the entire interview be transferred onto note cards? Should there be a bibliography card for the interview? If so, what information should be on it? Would the same hold true if you were using a survey instead of an interview?

5. You've never done research, and you're concerned about using direct and indirect quotes on your note cards. You're also really not sure how to paraphrase and would like to

practice this skill. You're not certain if direct quotes can be mixed with paraphrase. You need pointers on handling source material directly, indirectly, and in summary.

Exercise 4: Research Project—Writing Interview and Survey Questions

You've got the following problem:

1. You're studying the causes and effects of child abuse and you have the opportunity to interview a social worker who deals with abused children, an abusive parent, and an adult who was an abused child. Would it add to your information to interview all three? Should you ask them the same questions? What kinds of questions should you begin with? If you interview any of these people, how do you work the interview information into your paper? Do you need to use the entire interview in your finished project?

2. You're doing a survey of accounting students to see if they understand educational requirements, types of accountants, job responsibilities, salary range, and job potential. How should you set up your survey? What kinds of questions should you ask and in what order? How will you tabulate the results? How significant will your results be? Should you tell the accounting students the nature of your study before you give them the survey?

3. Your subject is runaway children. You've written interview questions that you want to ask the police officer who is head of the juvenile division. He is very cooperative and interested in what you're doing. You are both short of time. As you begin your questions, you find that he talks around the question and doesn't answer directly. Furthermore, he gives many long case histories that aren't related to what you're looking for. He also tends to get sidetracked and starts talking about juvenile delinquency. What should you do?

4. You've completed your survey and find that the results aren't what you expected. In fact, the results disprove your hypothesis. What kinds of things should you evaluate to decide if your survey or hypothesis needs revision? Must the survey data support your hypothesis if you are to use it?

5. You are interested in relating tales of UFO sightings in science fiction literature to the experiences of people who have seen UFO's. You are considering using a survey, but since you know some people who claim to have seen UFO's, you wonder if interviews might be more useful for your project. Can/should you use surveys and/or interviews? What kinds of questions should you ask? You also need help formulating unbiased questions. How can you tell if a question is biased and if it will elicit the kind of information you're looking for?

Exercise 5: Research Project—Writing That First Paragraph

Directions: All groups will work with the same problem.

You've got the following problem: you've done all your research and you're ready to write the research paper. You realize that the paper must be a continuous essay with a controlling idea and supporting ideas. You know that you must analyze your material, not just summarize it. But you just don't know how to write that first paragraph or two.

Your research question is "Are the Detroit police more/less tolerant toward marijuana users than suburban police?" You have done an extensive survey of the Detroit Police Narcotics Bureau and of the police in a nearby suburb. You have also interviewed the department head of the Detroit and suburban bureaus. You have found some related written material, but not much. You've decided to use a short story, "A Policeman's Journal," by T. Mike Walker, to illustrate police attitudes and training.

Since there is no room to reproduce all the materials you have found, the group may make up any approach and information necessary to write the first (and second) paragraph for this paper.

Exercise 6: Research Project—Footnotes and Bibliography

Directions: All groups will work with the same problem.

You've got the following problem: you have decided to use a separate page for footnotes instead of placing them at the bottom of appropriate pages. You've got a problem with form. How would you arrange the following in acceptable form for footnote and bibliography pages?

Here is the necessary information for the footnote page in the order that each reference appears in the paper.

a. An educational attitude survey you conducted of 50 DIT freshmen on March 15, 1978. Since you often refer to the survey later in the paper, you'd like to find some way to avoid using a footnote each time you refer to it.

b. A television news report entitled "The Quality of Education" on Channel 2 at 11:00 on March 5, 1978. It was delivered by Robbie Timmons.

c. *The Detroit News* ran an article "SAT Test Results" on March 7, 1978, page 3C. No author was given.

d. *Curriculum Development* is a book written by Daniel Tanner and Laurel Tanner. It was published in New York by Macmillan Publishing Co., Inc., in 1975. Page 25.

e. The book is *The City Today* edited by George L. Groman. It was published by Harper & Row in New York, 1978. The essay you are referring to is "The Role of the Teacher" written by Fillmore K. Peltz. The page is 222.

f. You refer again to Tanner and Tanner's book.

g. An interview you conducted with John Smith, the principal of Detroit's Riverside High School on March 10, 1978. However, he does not want his name or high school mentioned.

Using the information provided in the footnotes, write a bibliography.

Exercise 7: Research Project—Appendixes

Directions: All groups will work with the same problem.

You've got the following problem: you haven't included the following in the body of your paper.

a. The method(s) used in your surveys or interviews. The strengths and weaknesses of your method(s). Suggestions you'd make to future students who would like to repeat and/or add to your study.

b. The complete text of the interview(s). If these interviews are on tape, should they be transcribed? Are there other alternatives?

c. Suggestions for related studies that you thought of while doing your research.

d. Statistics and charts that relate to your topic but that didn't belong in the body of the paper.

e. A copy of your interview questions and/or survey form.

Yet, you think this material is important and should be included with your project. Is this material really useful to a reader? Why or why not? Can it be included in the appendix? If so, how should it be set up and in what order should it appear? Are the appendixes ever mentioned in the body of the paper? If so, how and when?

Exercise 8: Research Project—Evaluation

Directions: All groups will work with the same problem.

You have the following problem: you've worked hard and you're wondering if it's all been worthwhile. How good is your project? What would you do differently? The same? You're trying to decide what, if anything, you've learned about yourself and others. What you've learned, if anything, about research, writing, thinking, and/or reading?

Summary

Throughout the exercises, students had to consider questions from many points of view. They had to use both objective and subjective evidence. They experienced the frustrations of trying to analyze and unify this mass of material. They began investigating instead of just compiling and repeating facts. In fact, the assignment was much more difficult than the traditional research paper. But the students really learned. They found that they were able to solve their own research problems. And when they couldn't, they welcomed proposals from others. Students began to work more cooperatively and became more involved in helping their classmates. In short, they learned a multitude of research techniques as well as the satisfaction of active cooperation.

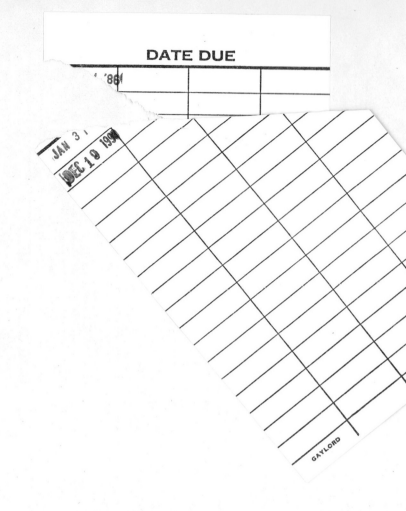